I0499687

If Lost, Please Return To:

Name:______________________

Phone:______________________

Email:______________________

Color Test Page

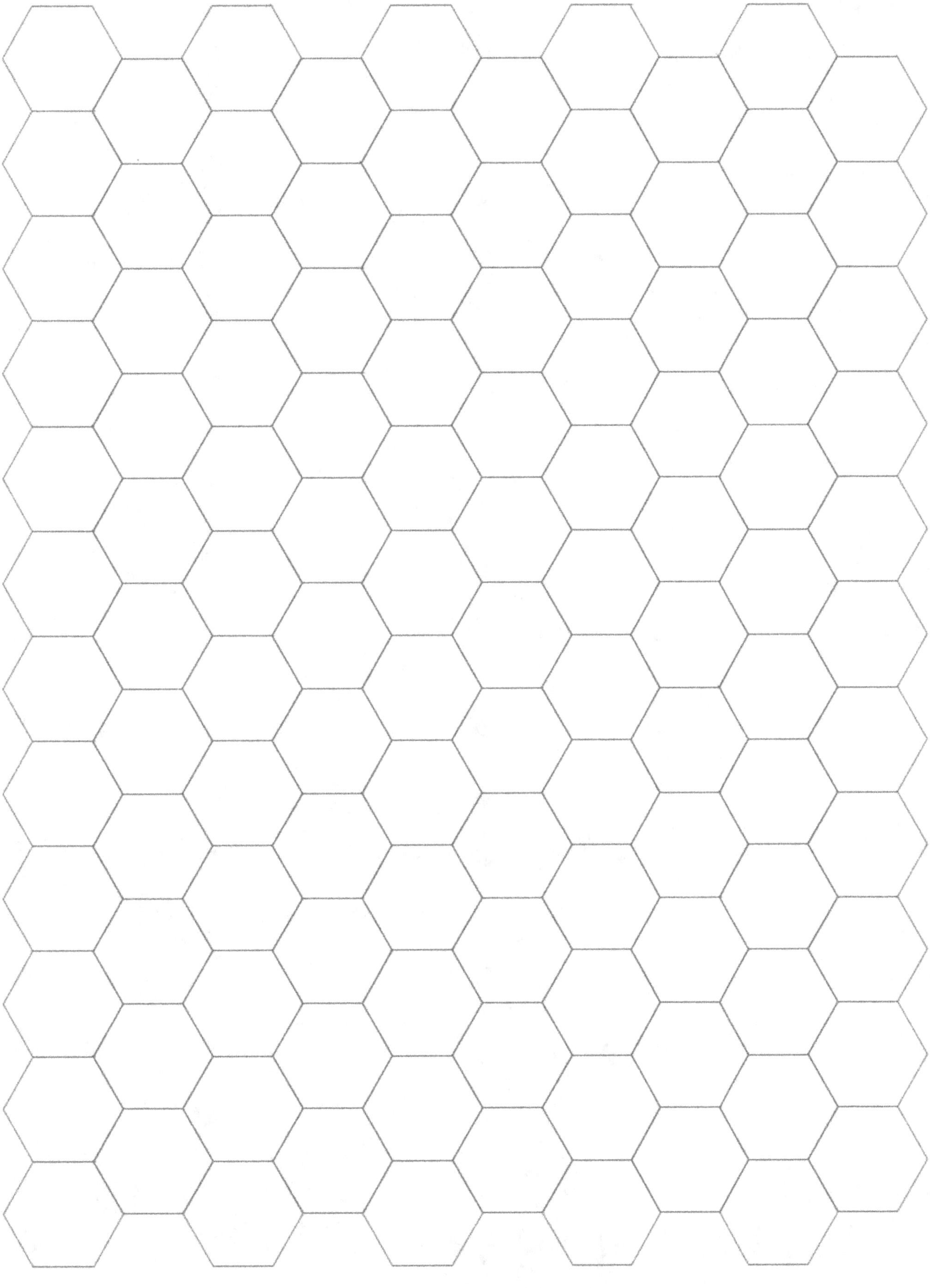

Color Test Page

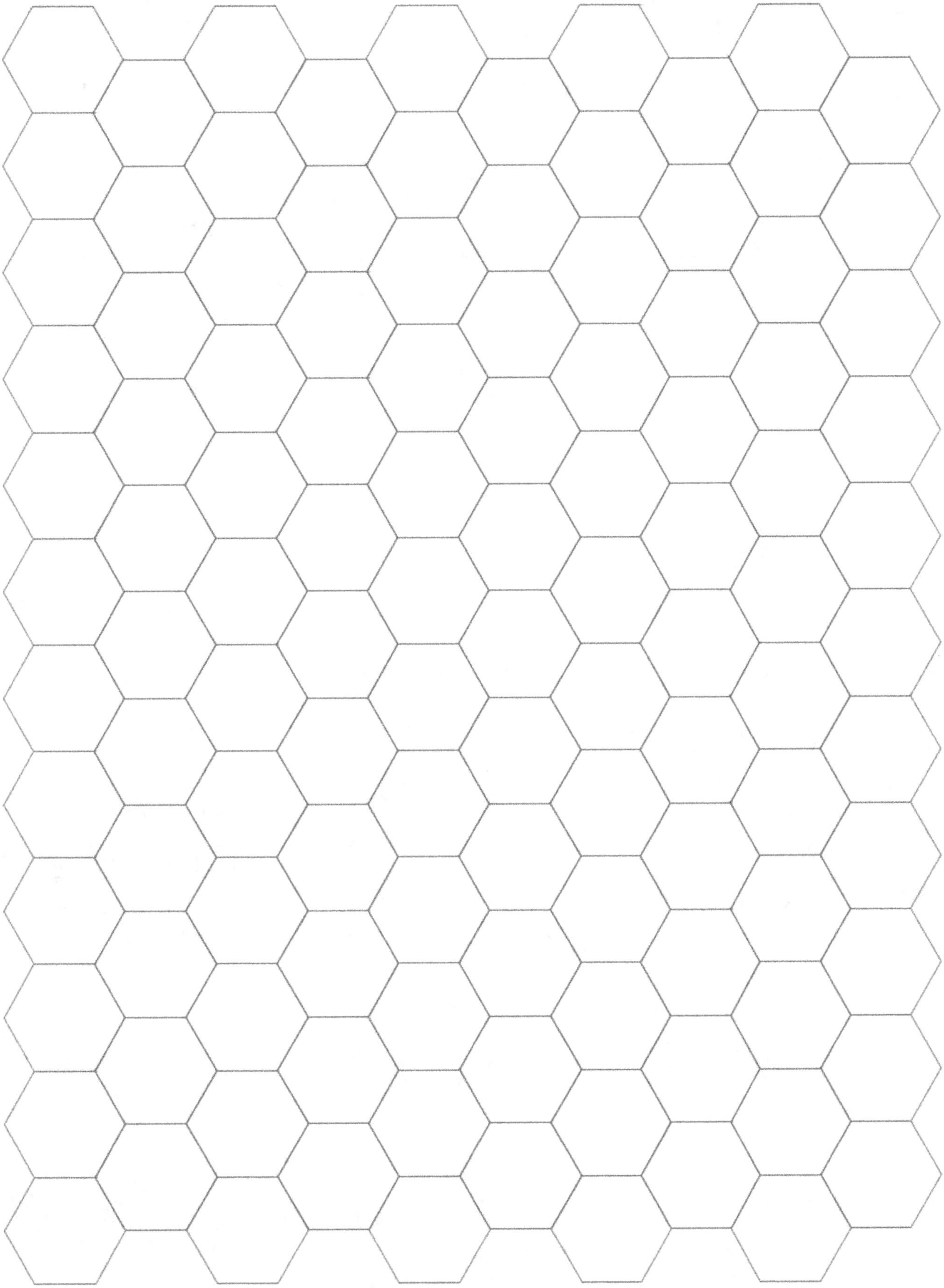

Color Test Page

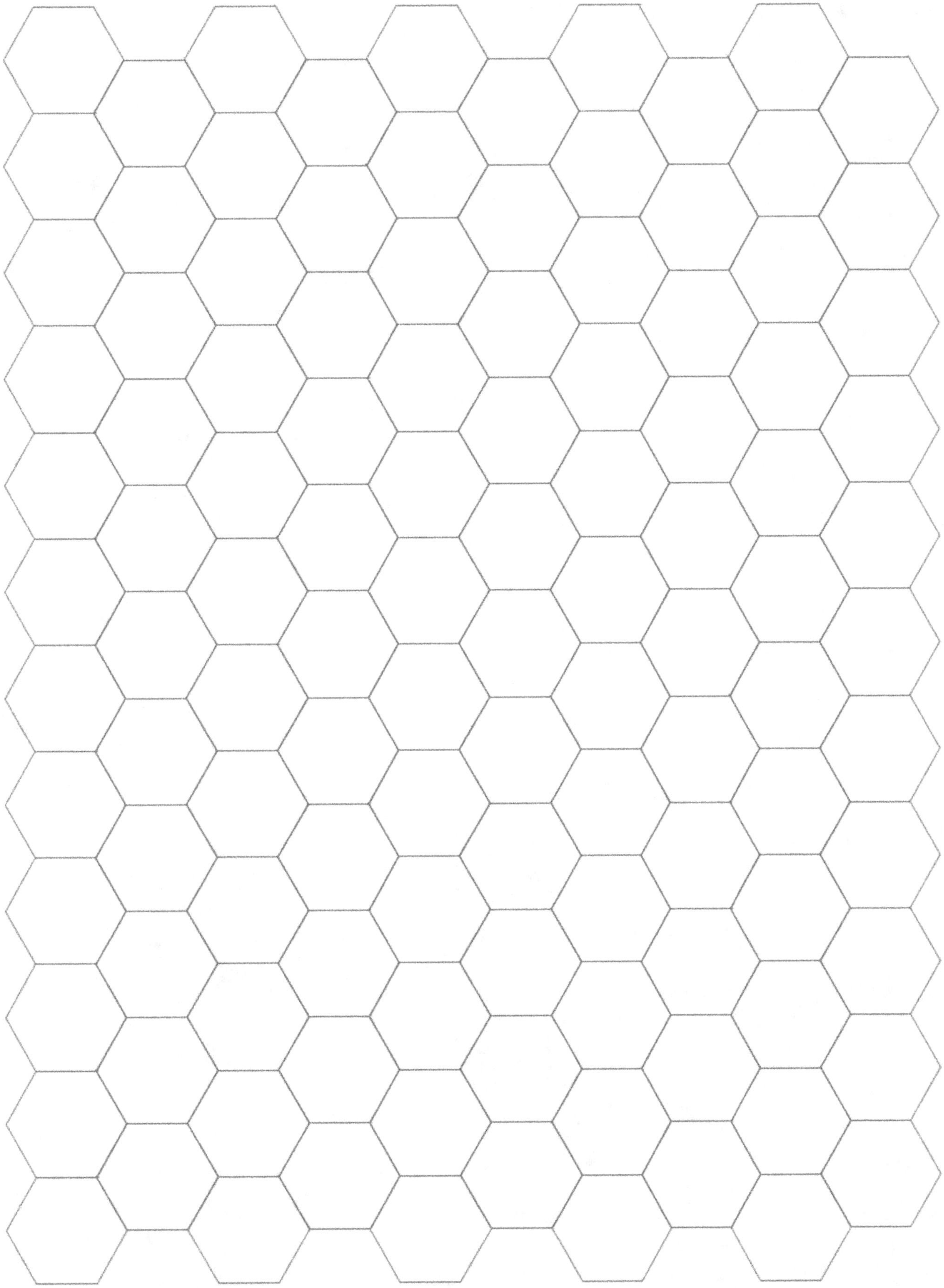

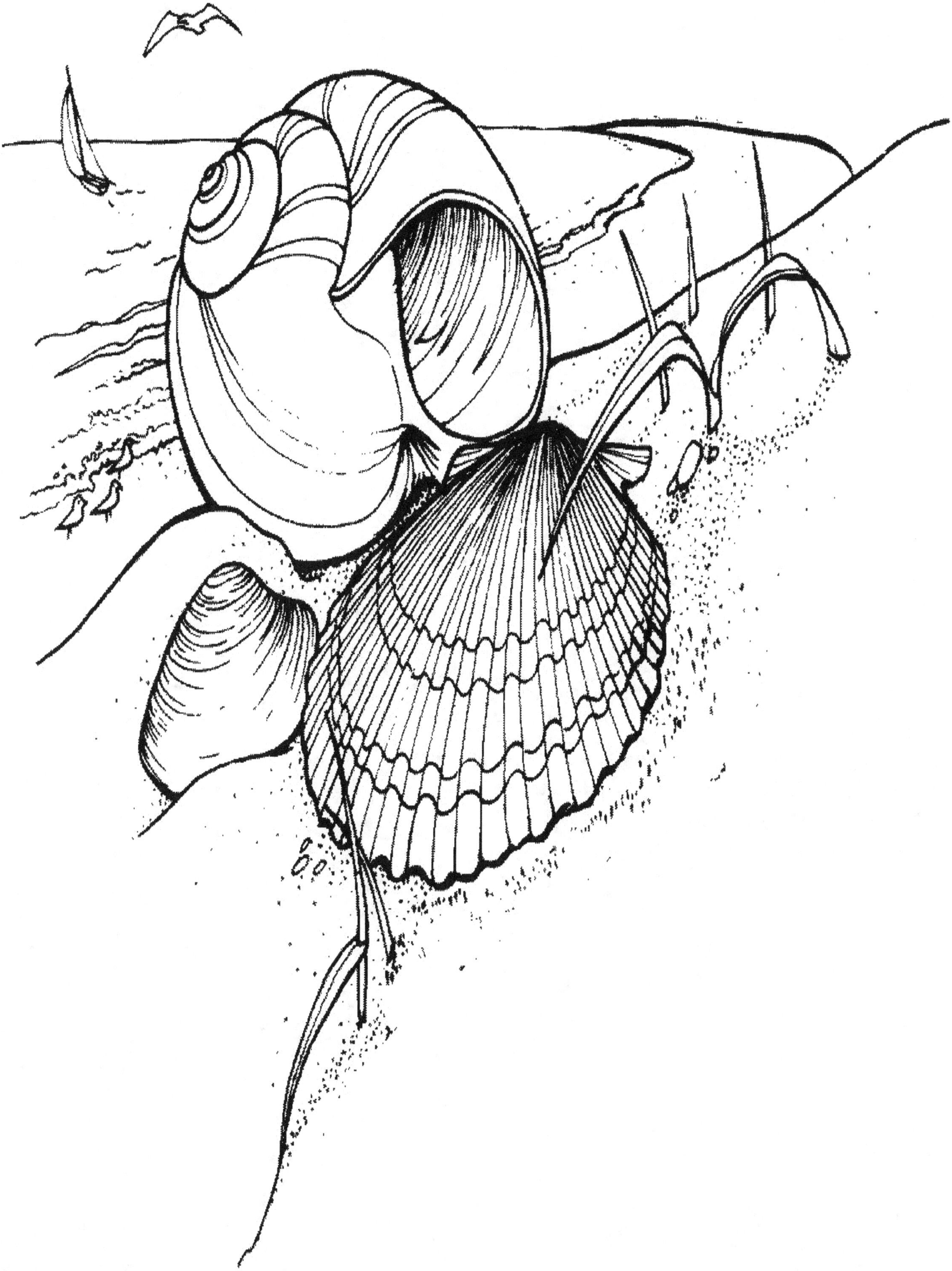

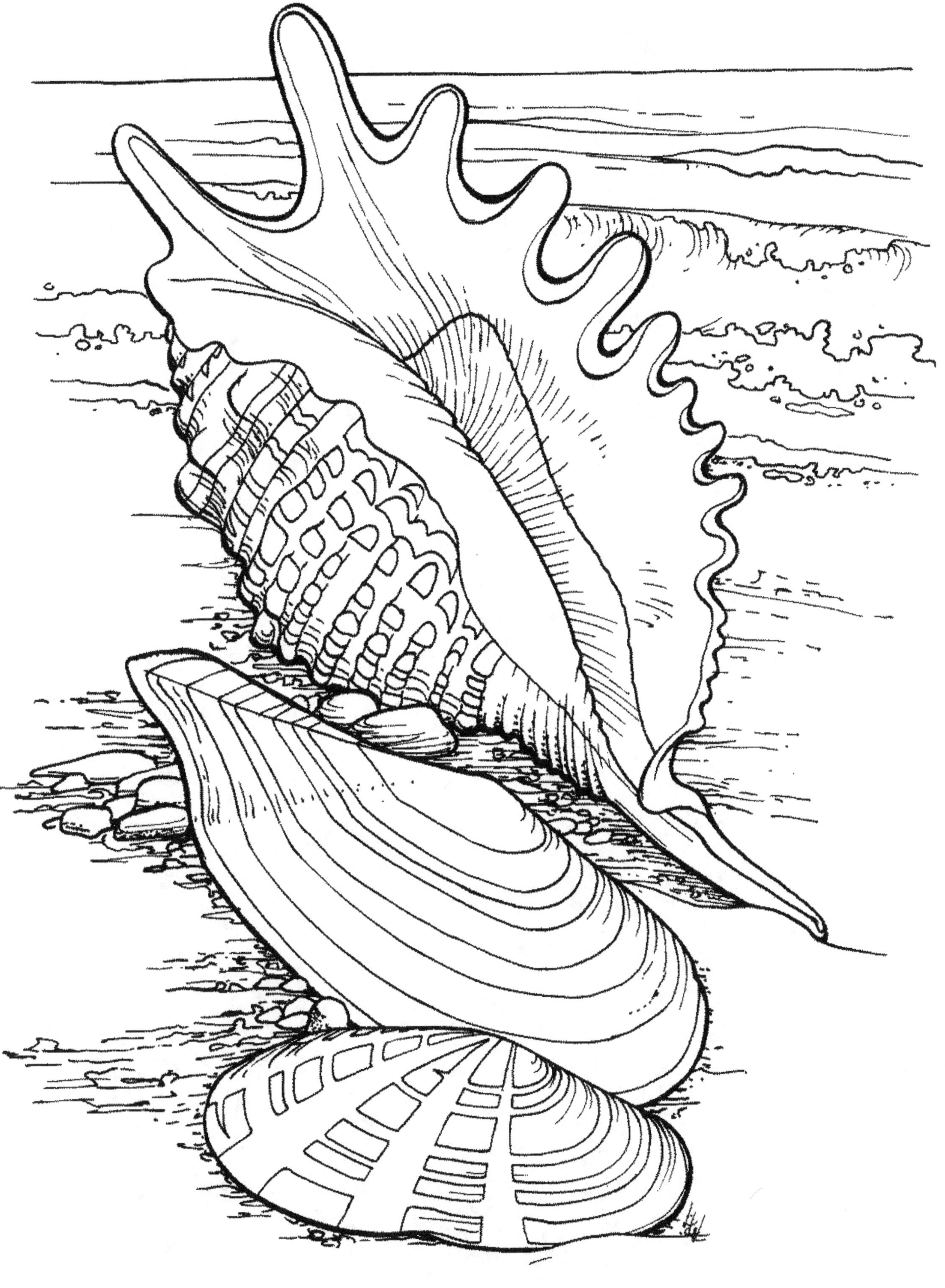

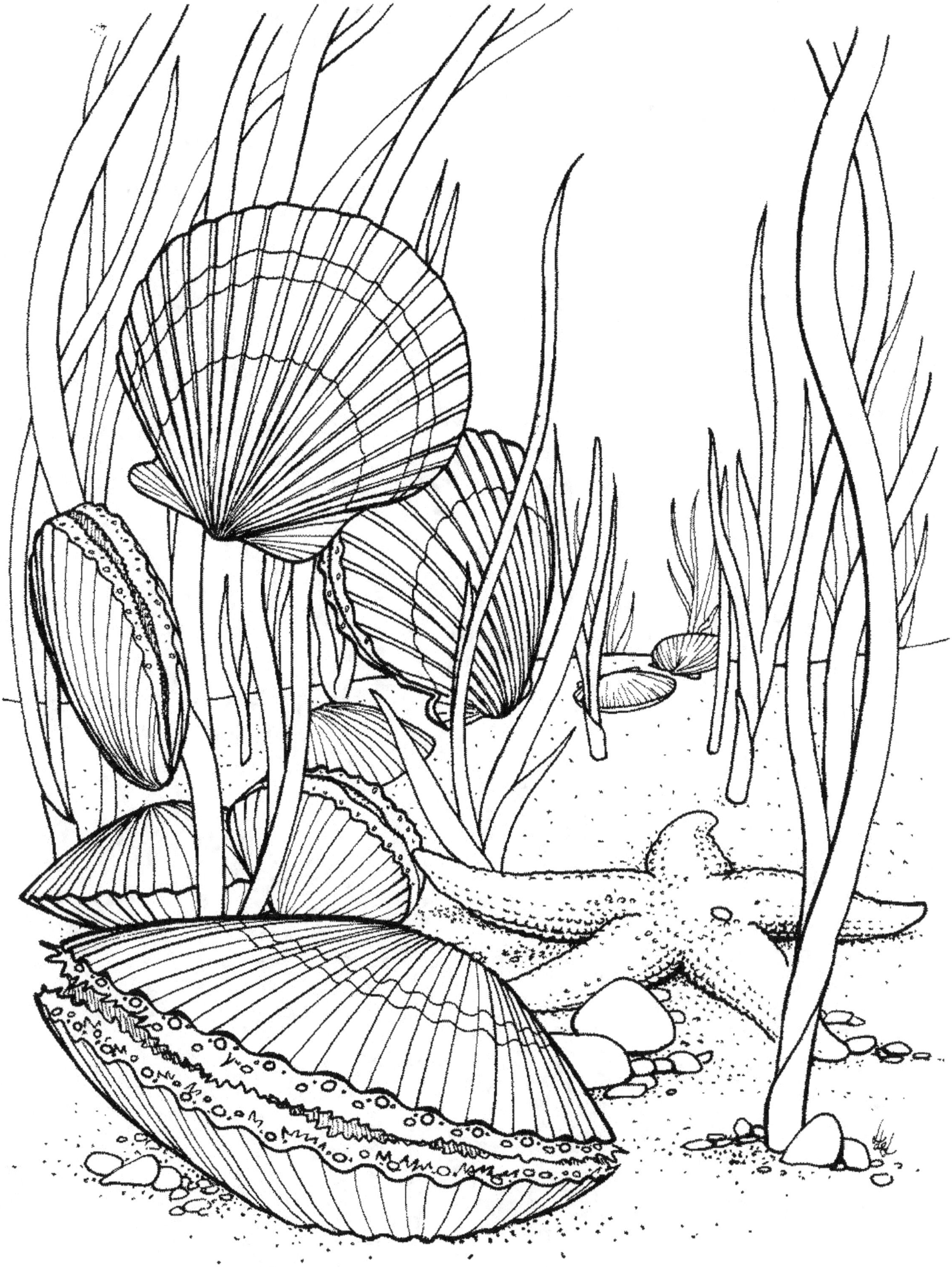

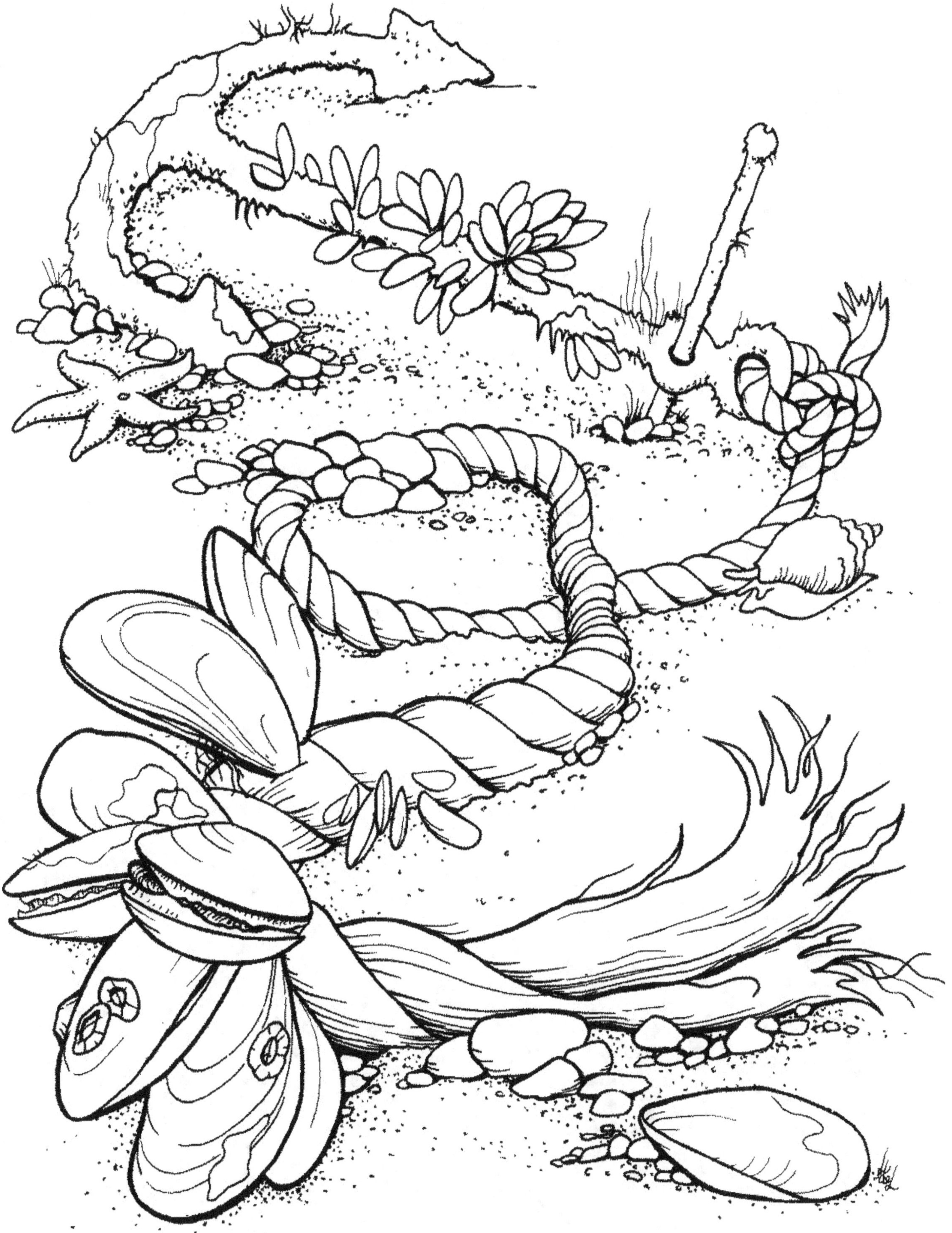

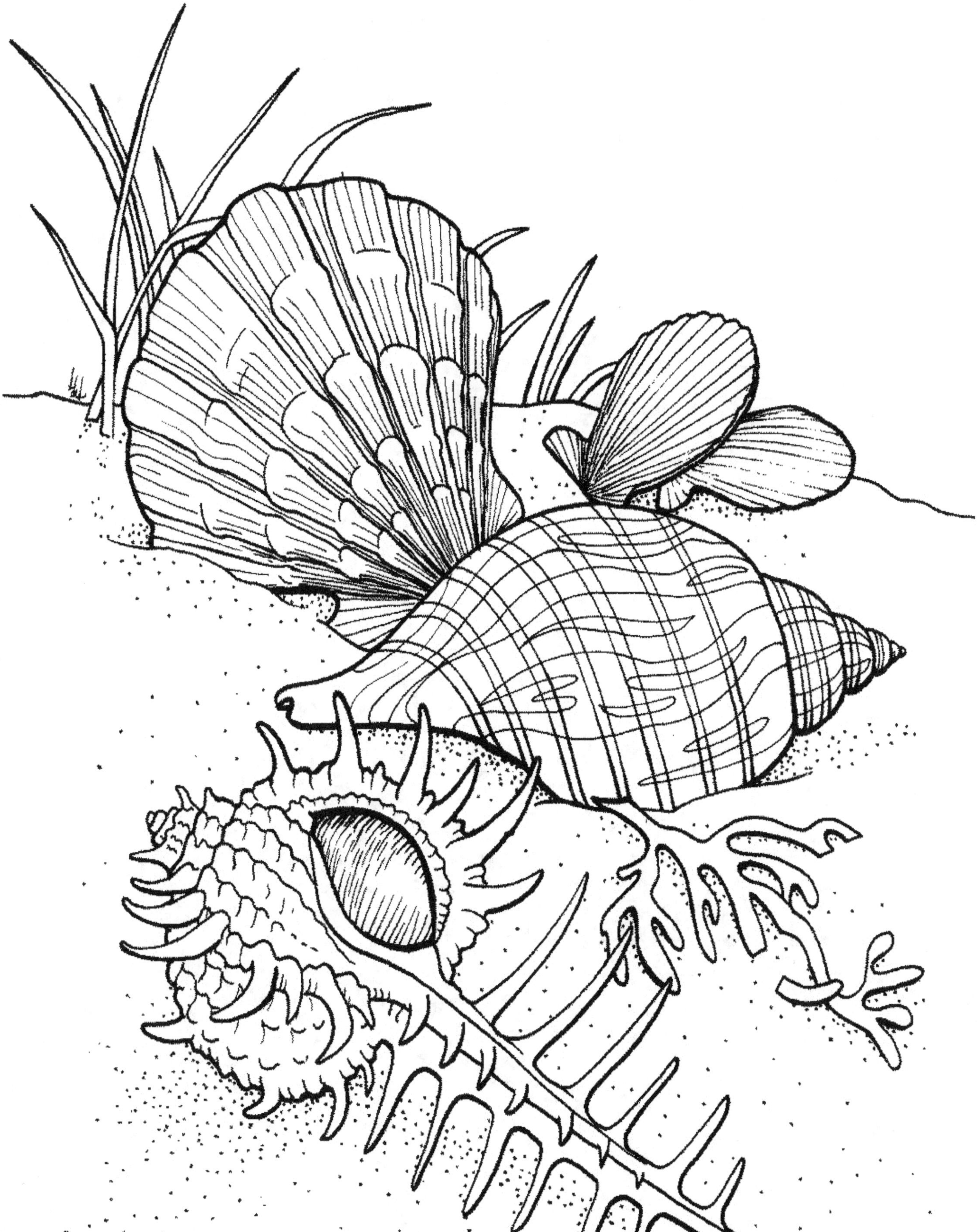

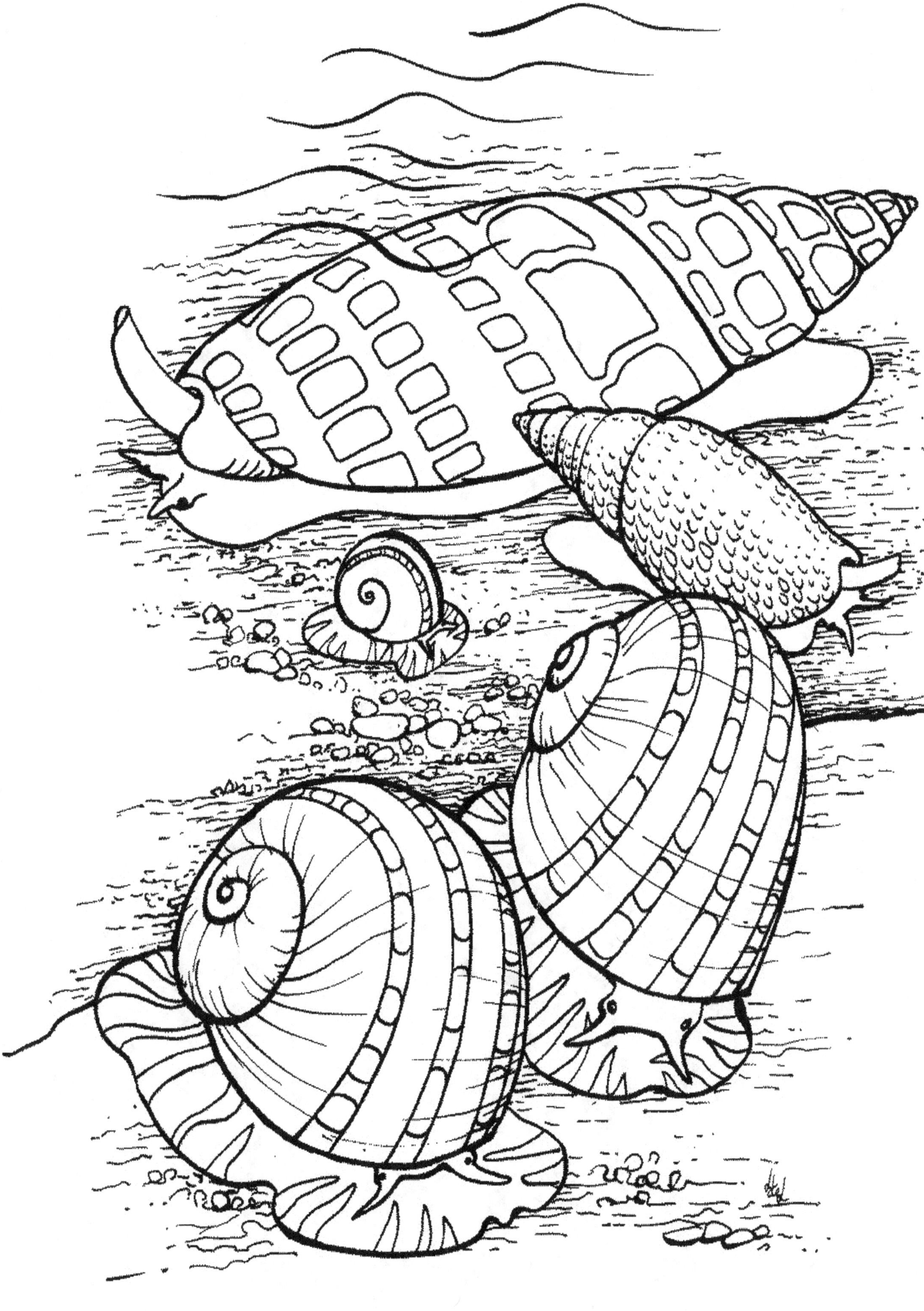

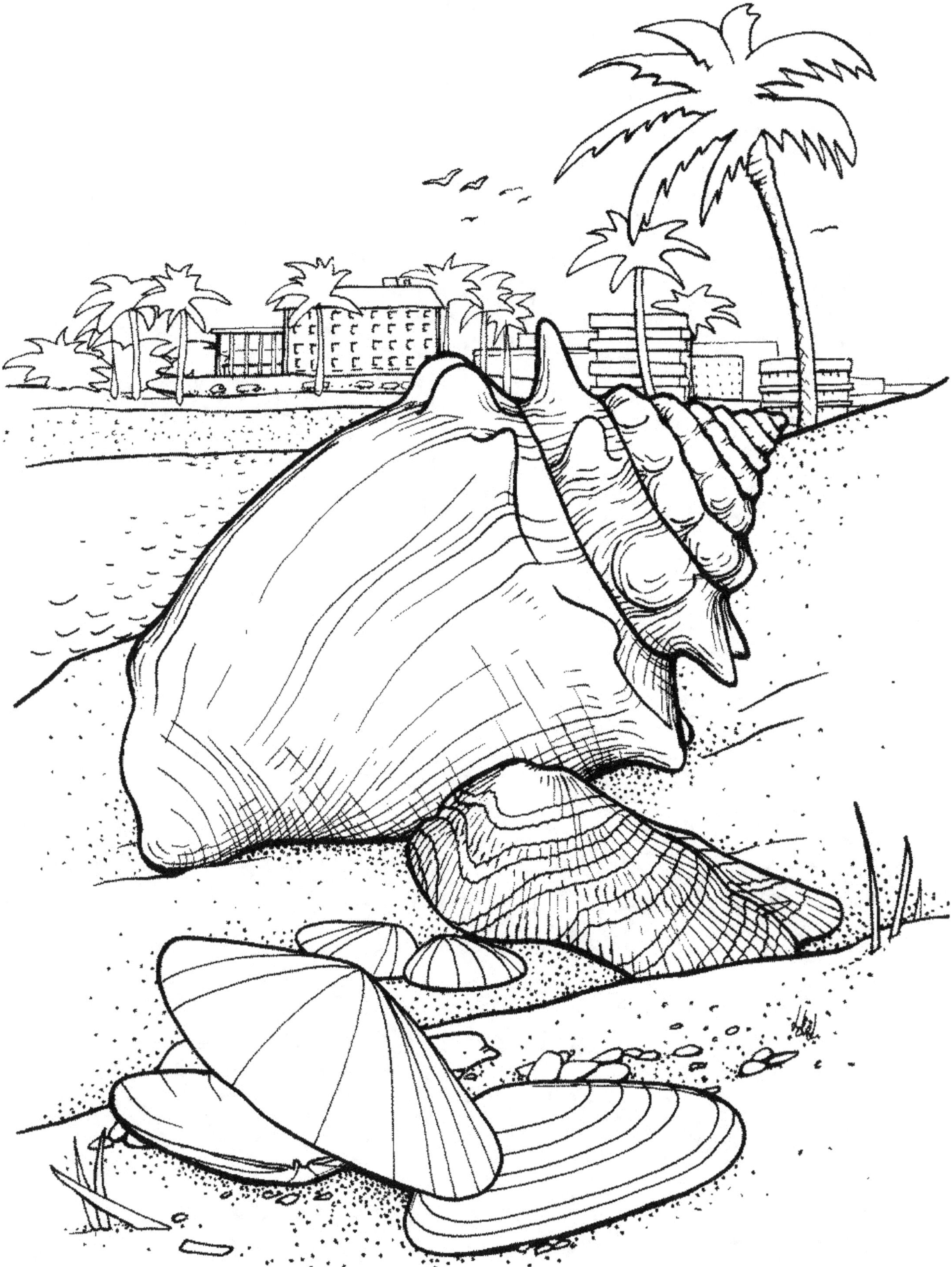

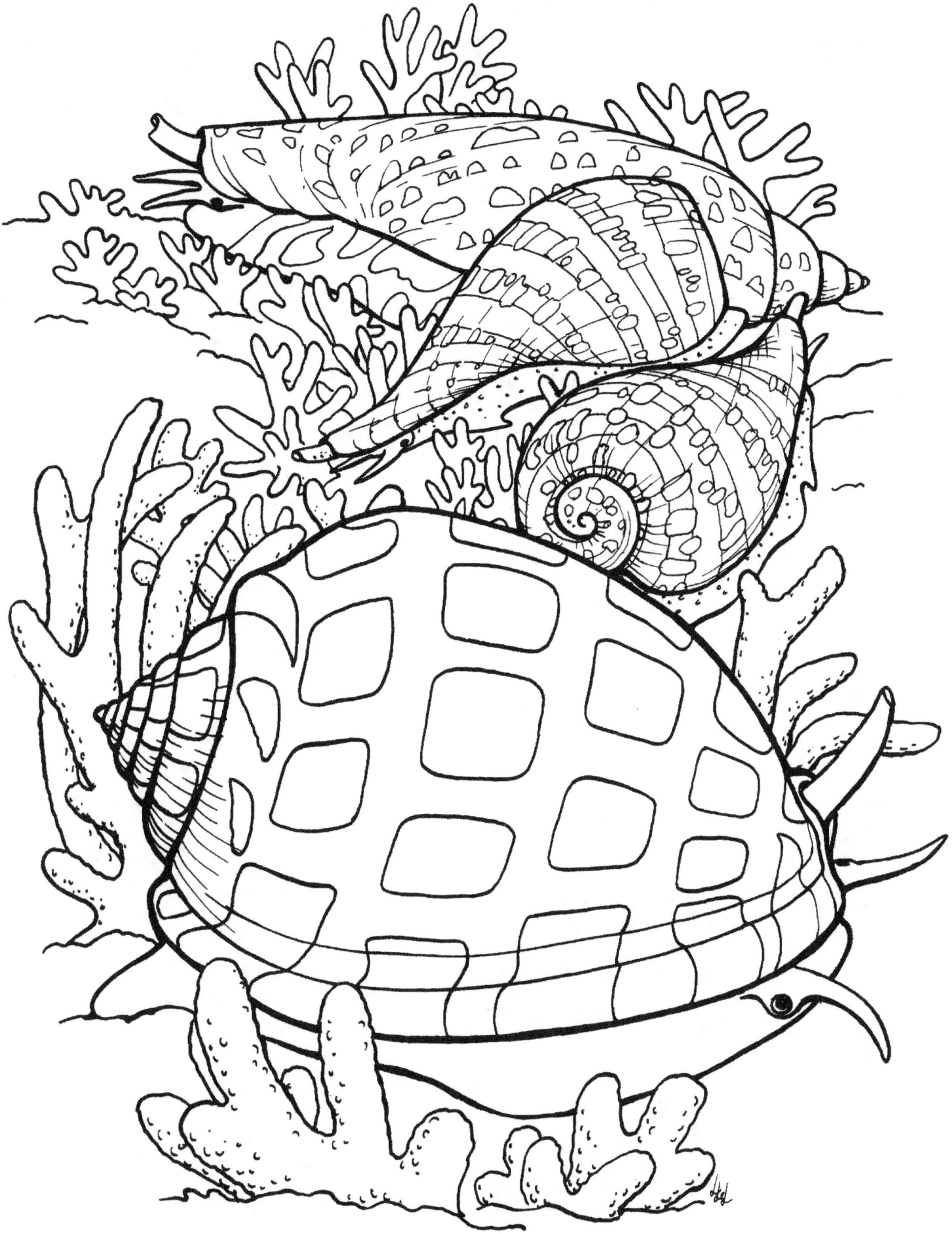

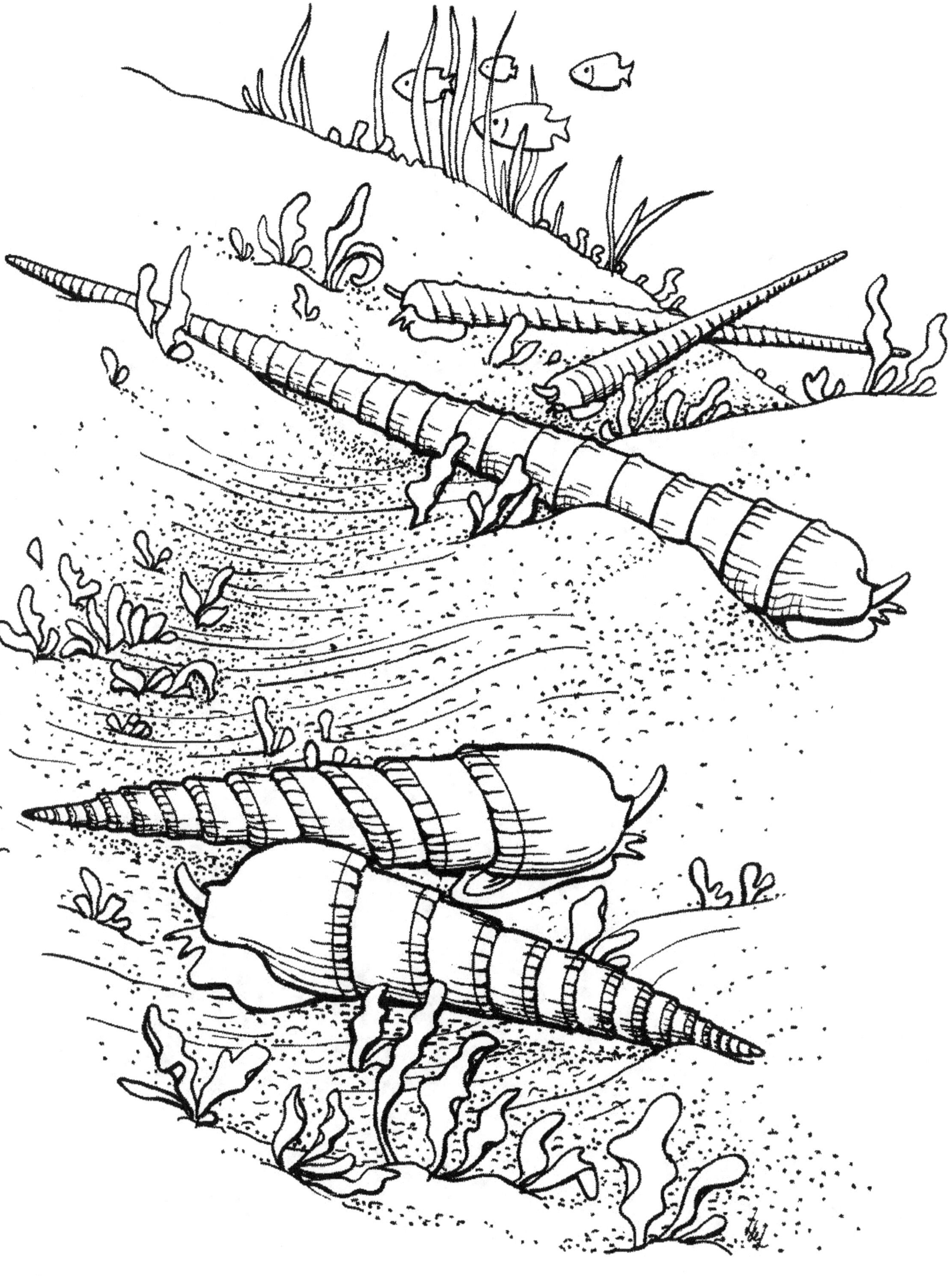

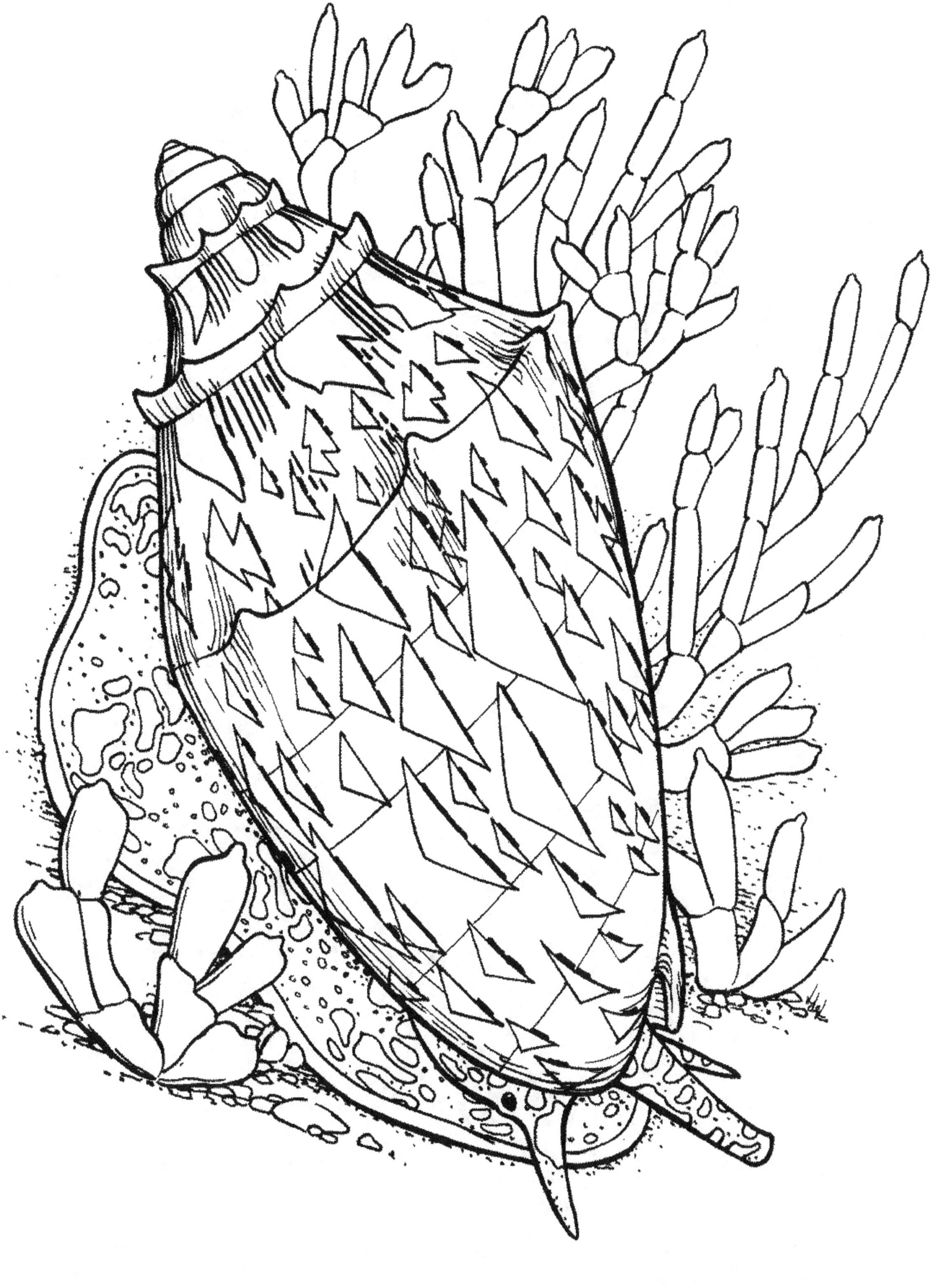

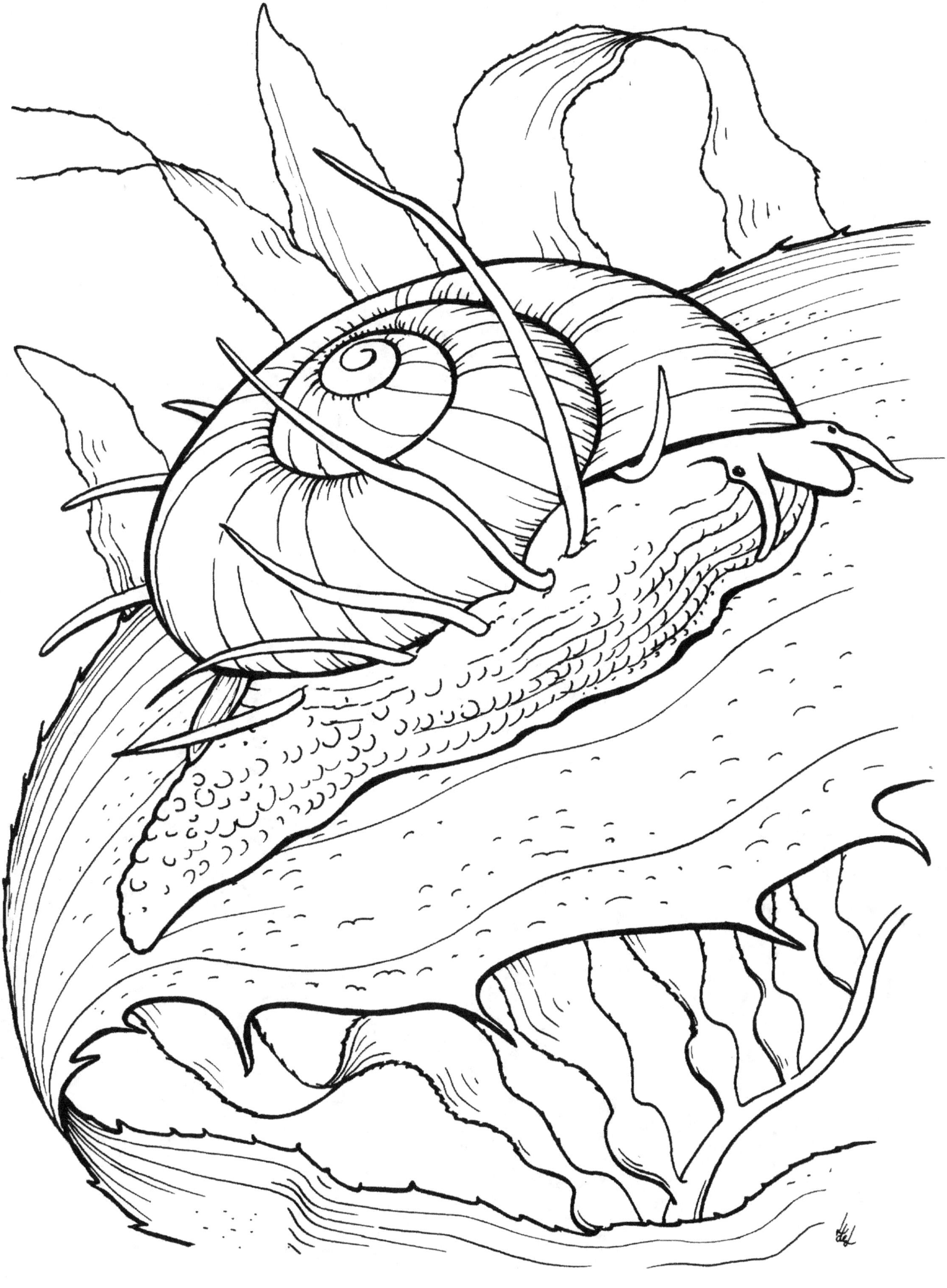

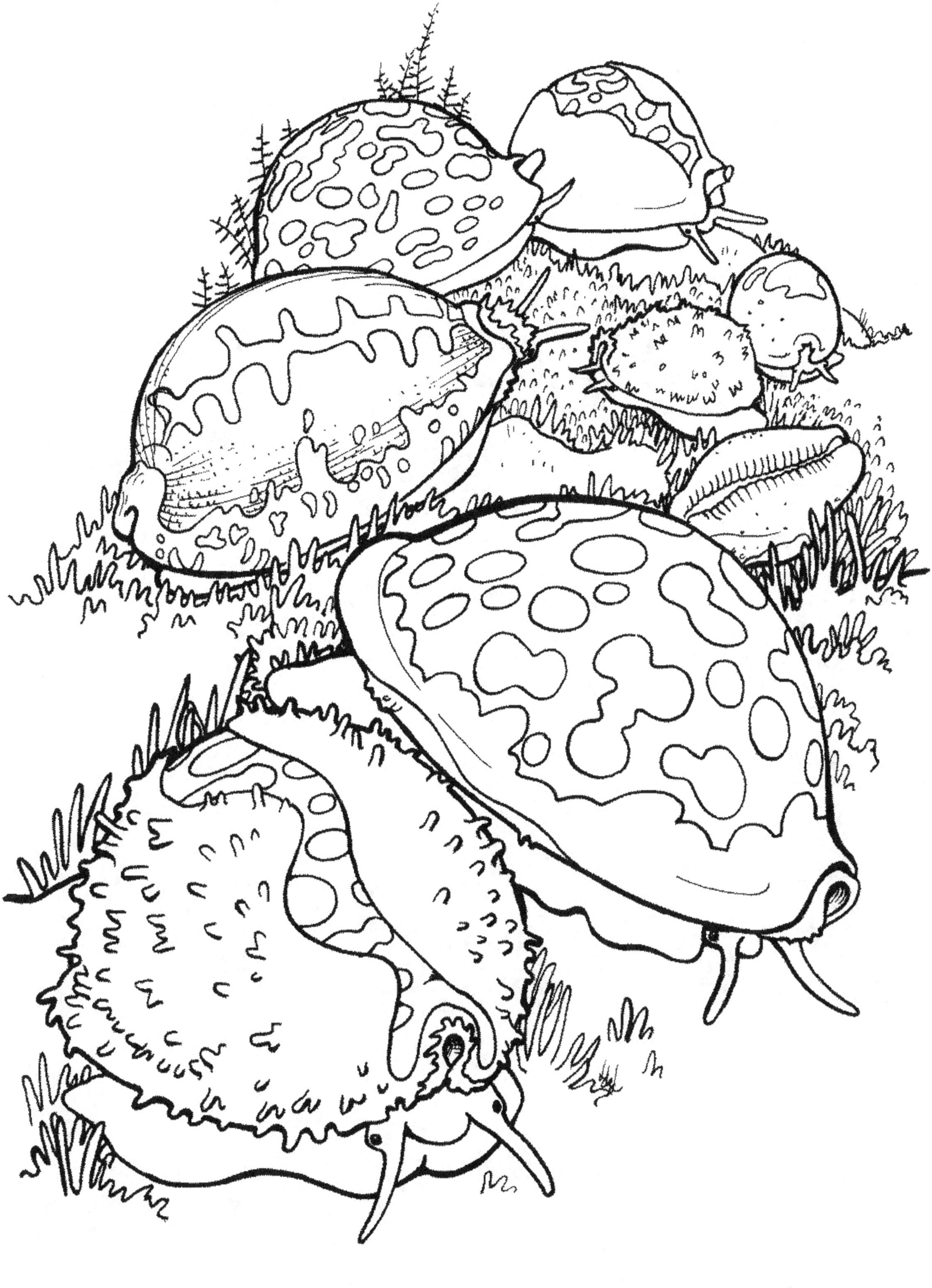

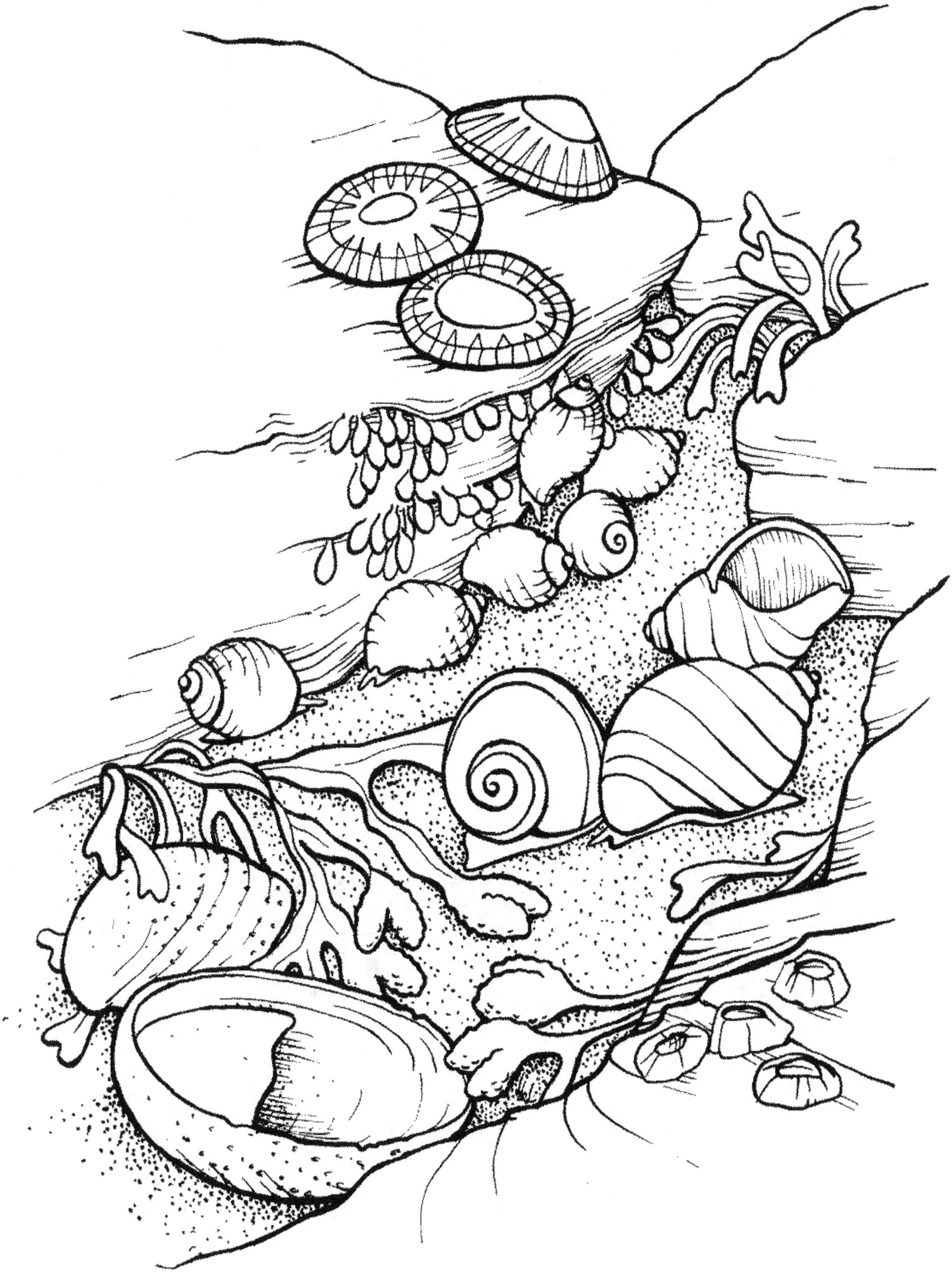

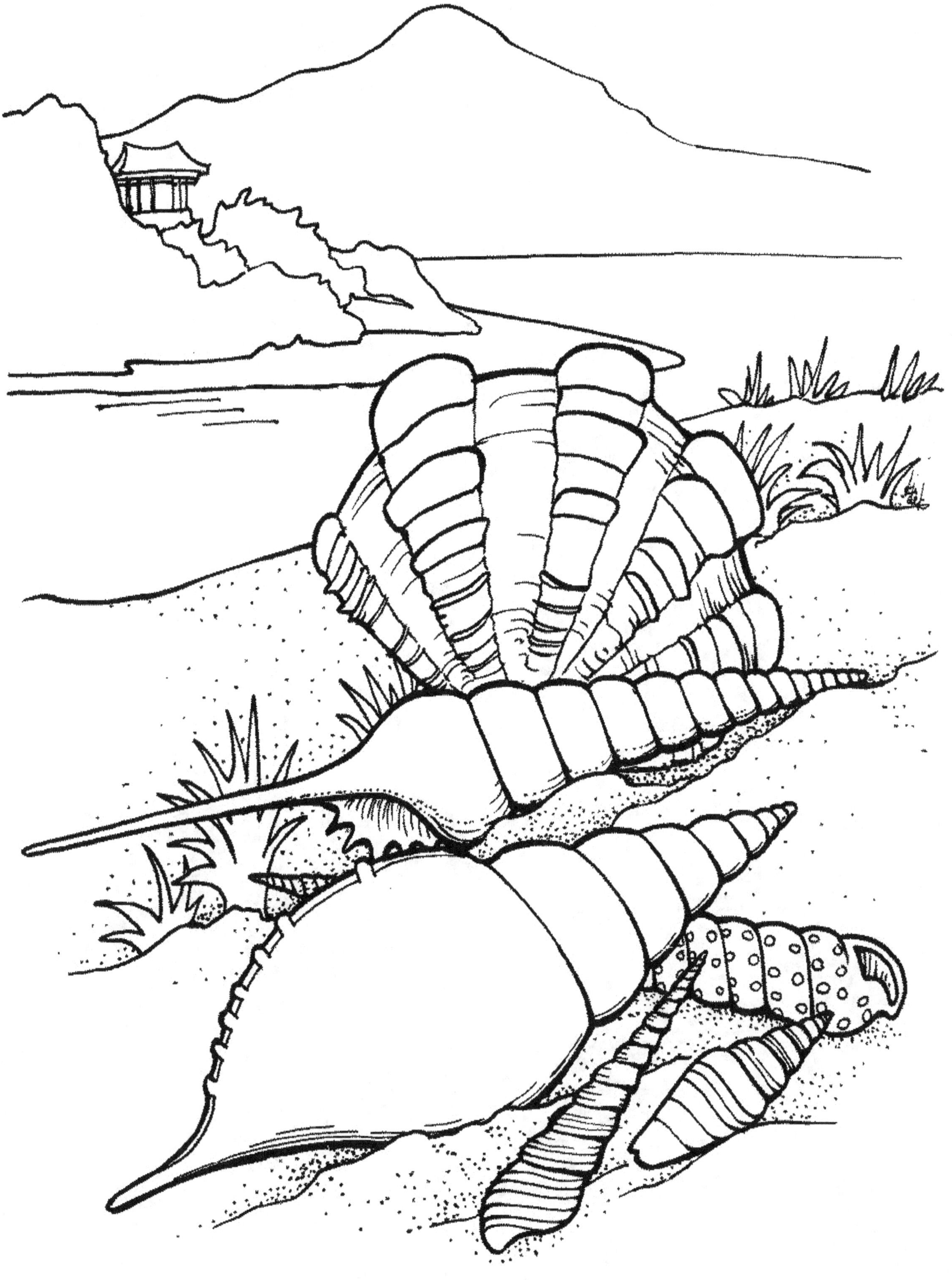

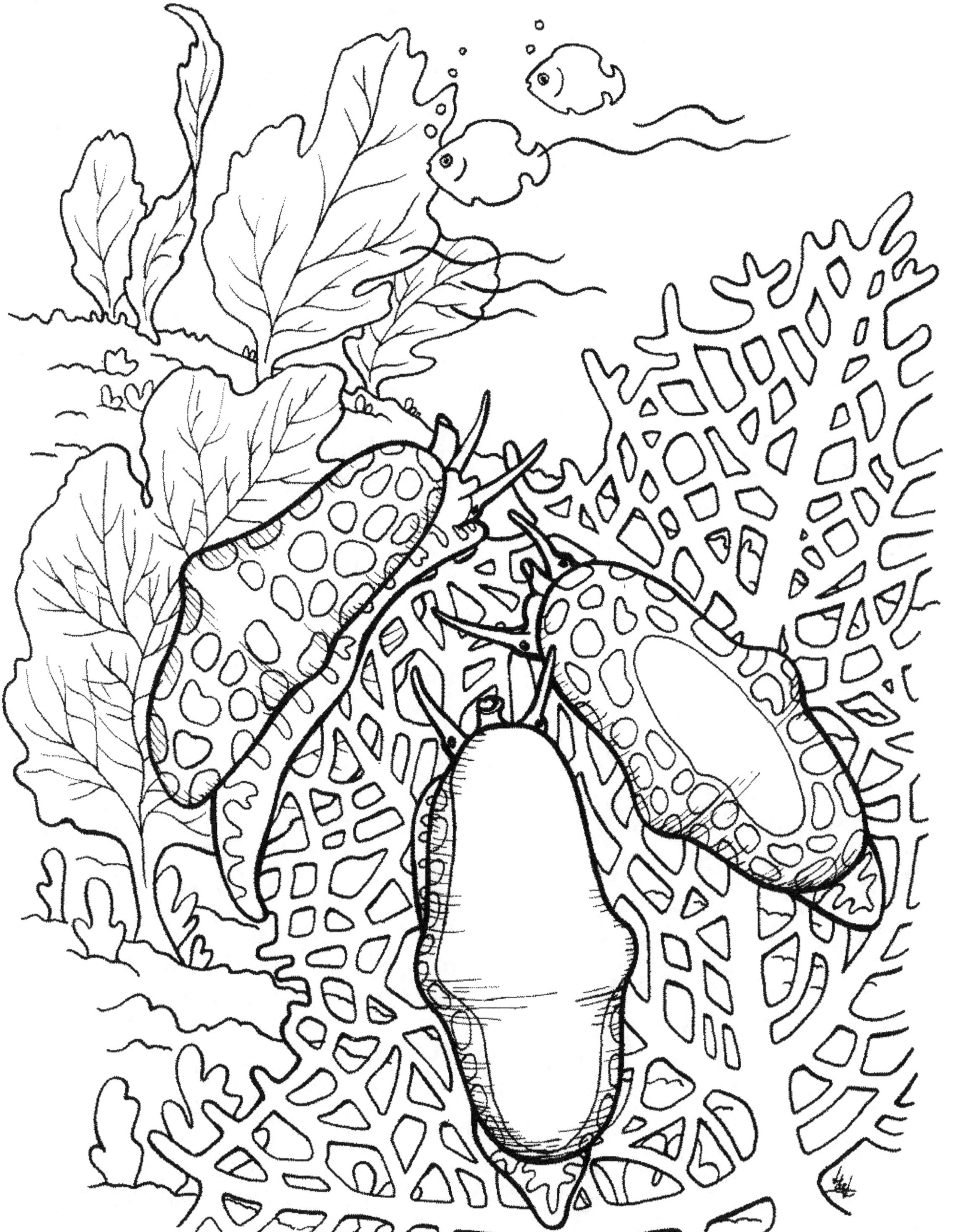

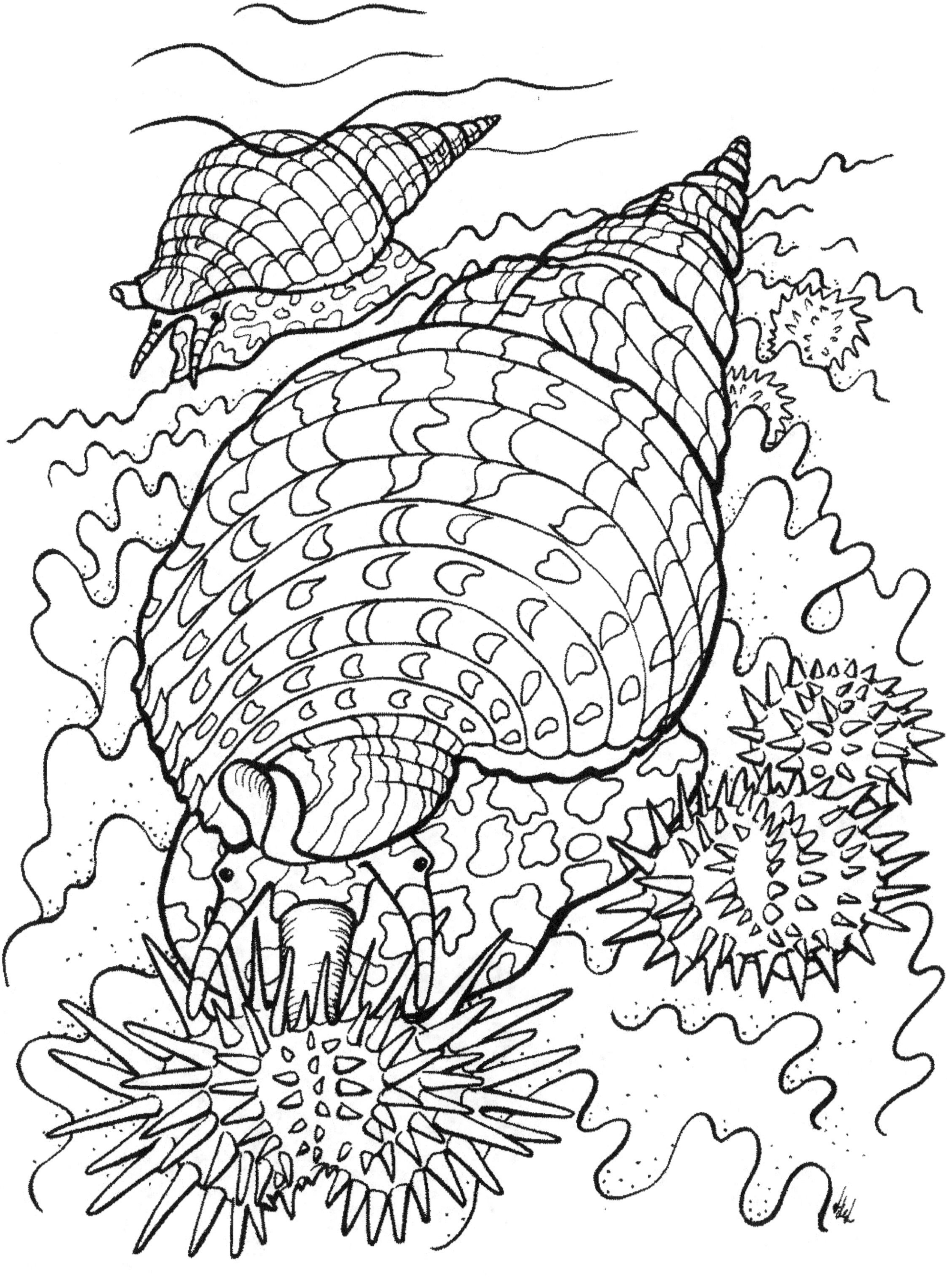

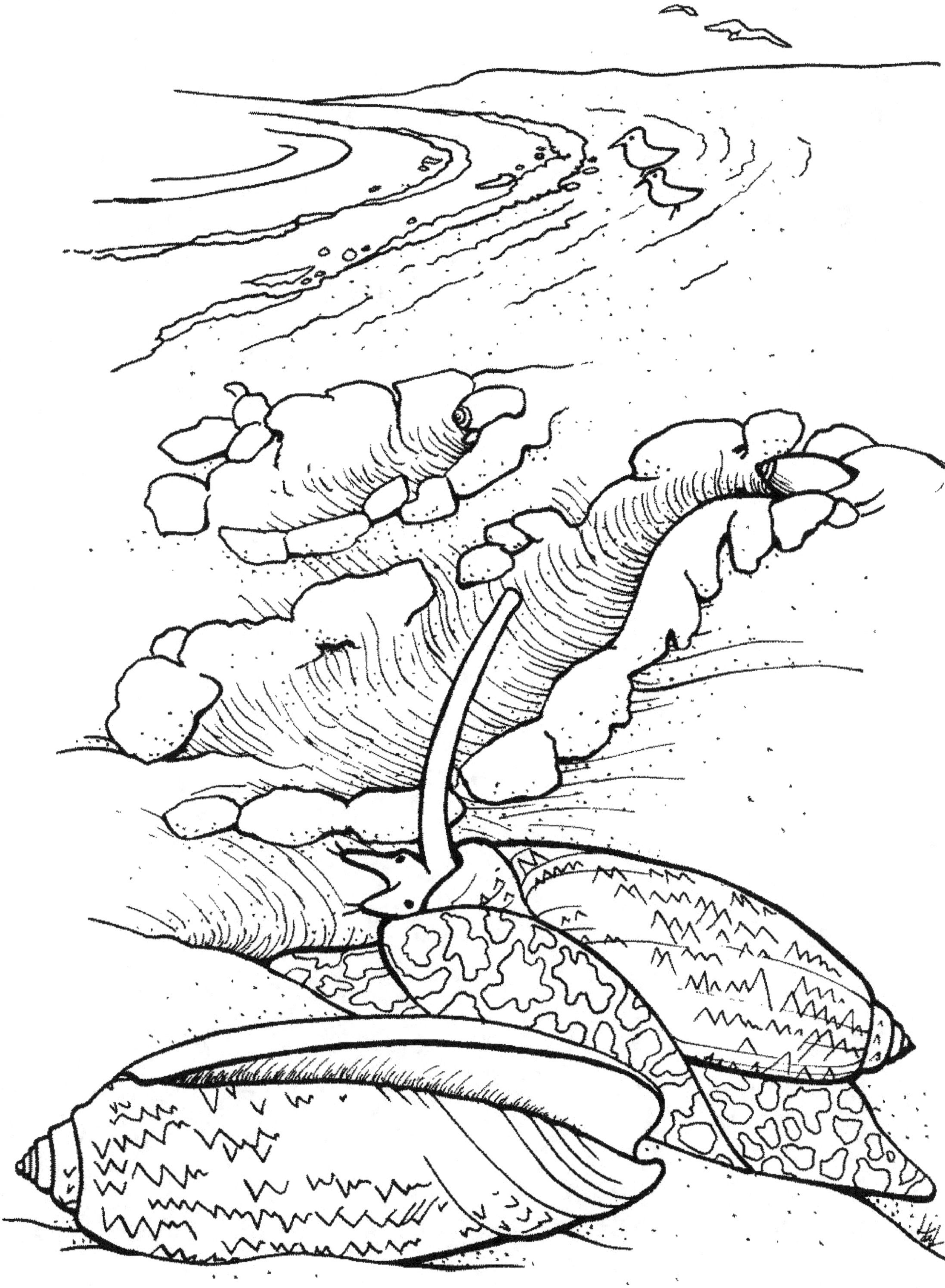

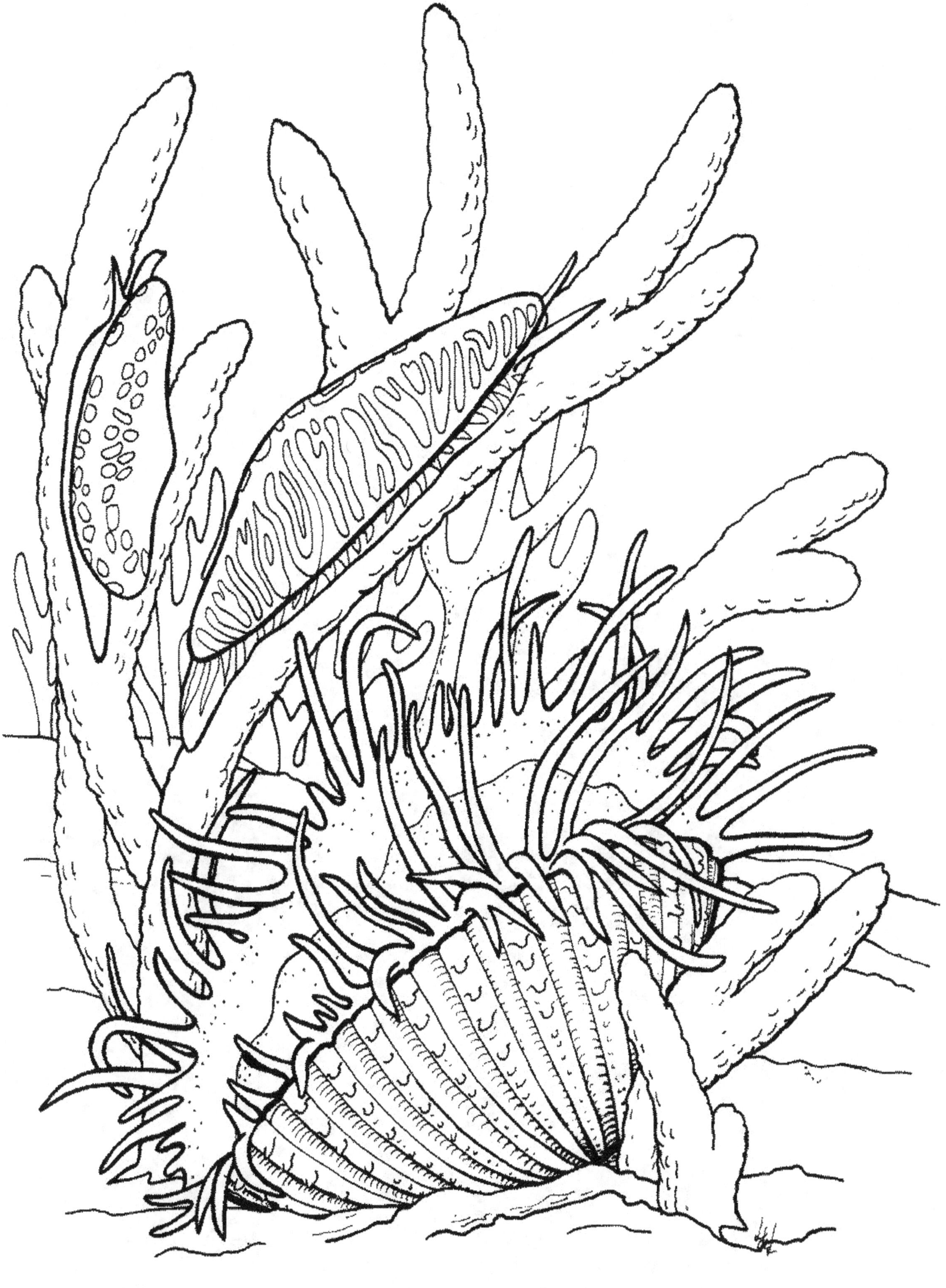

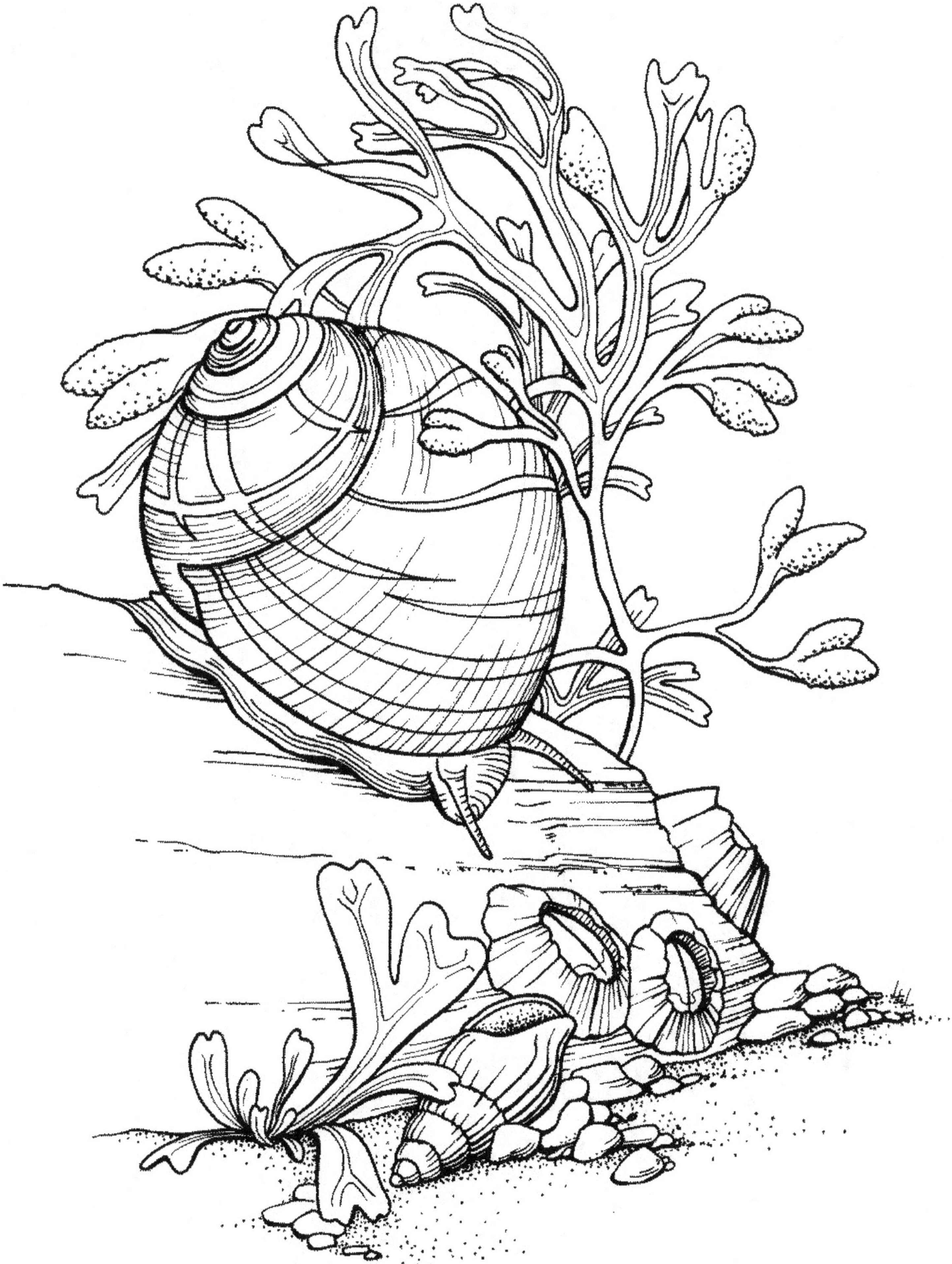

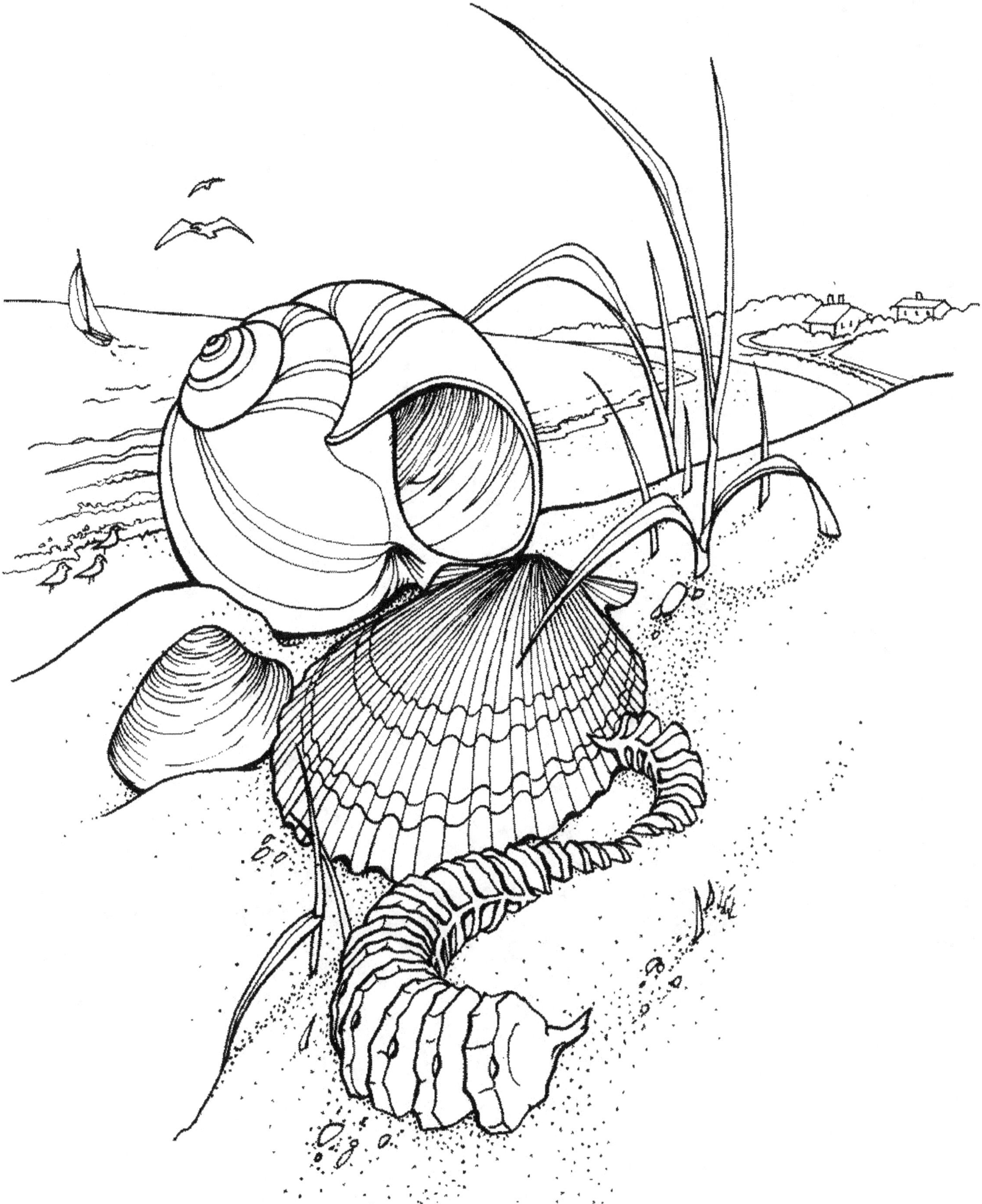

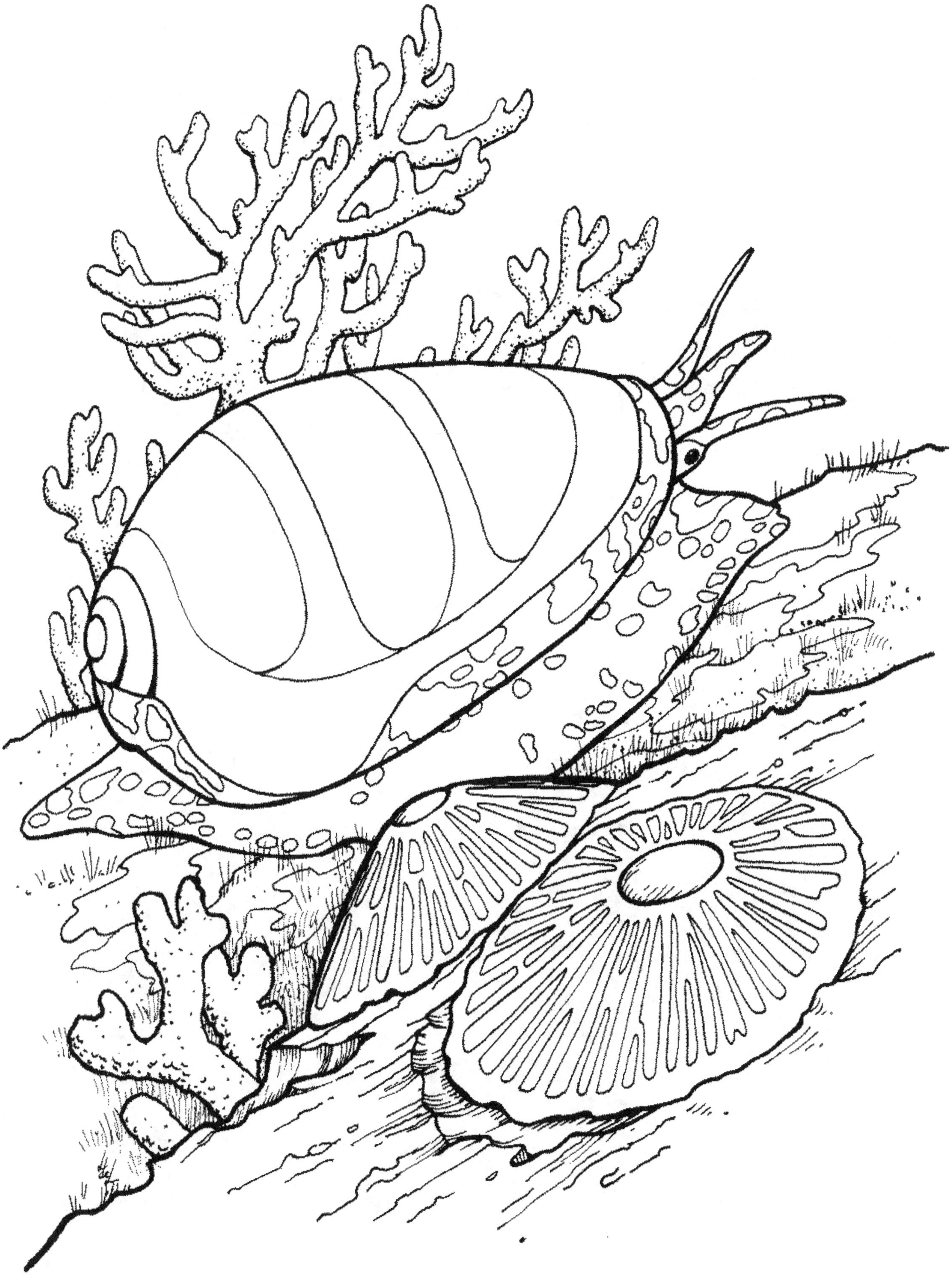

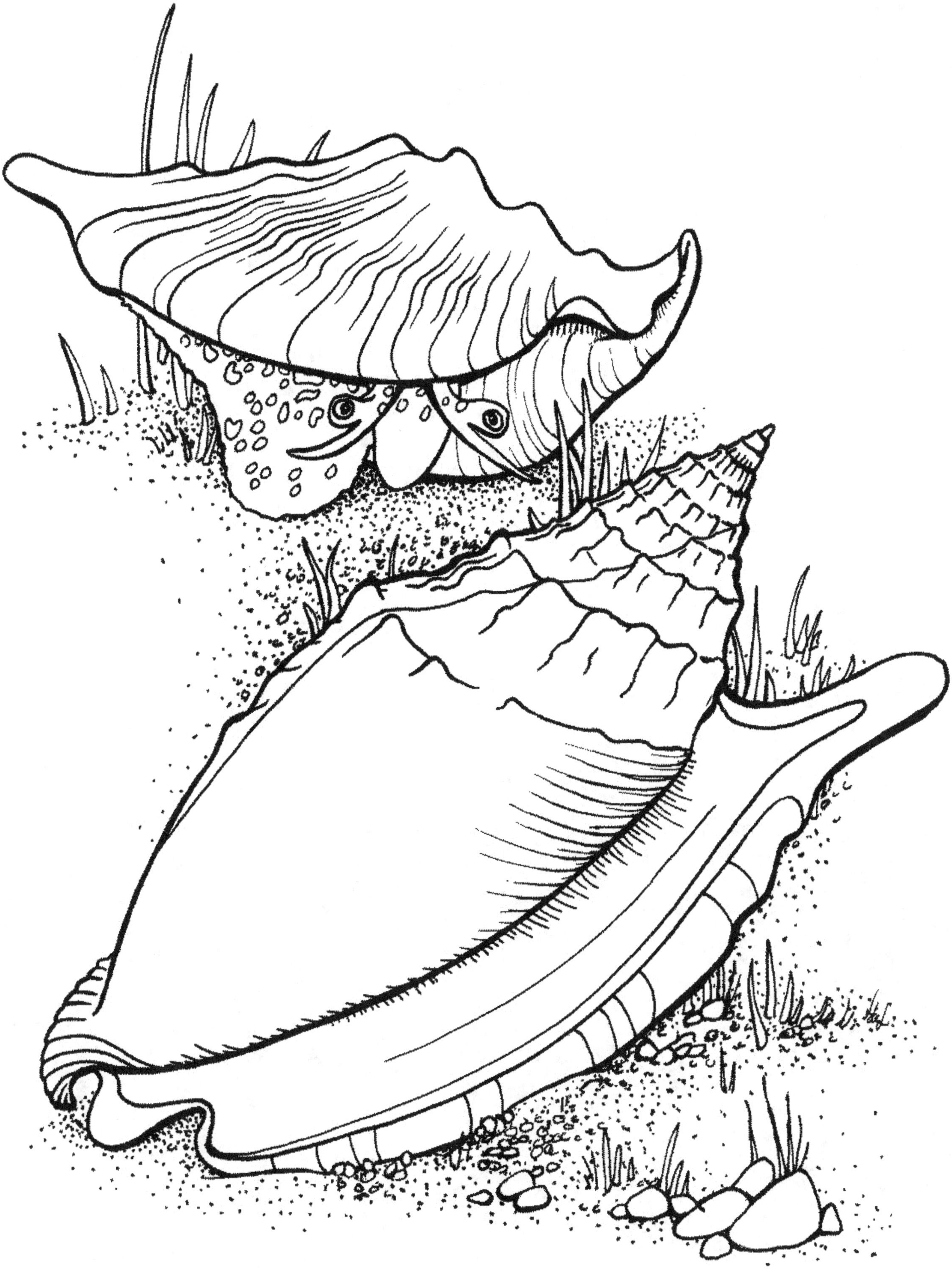

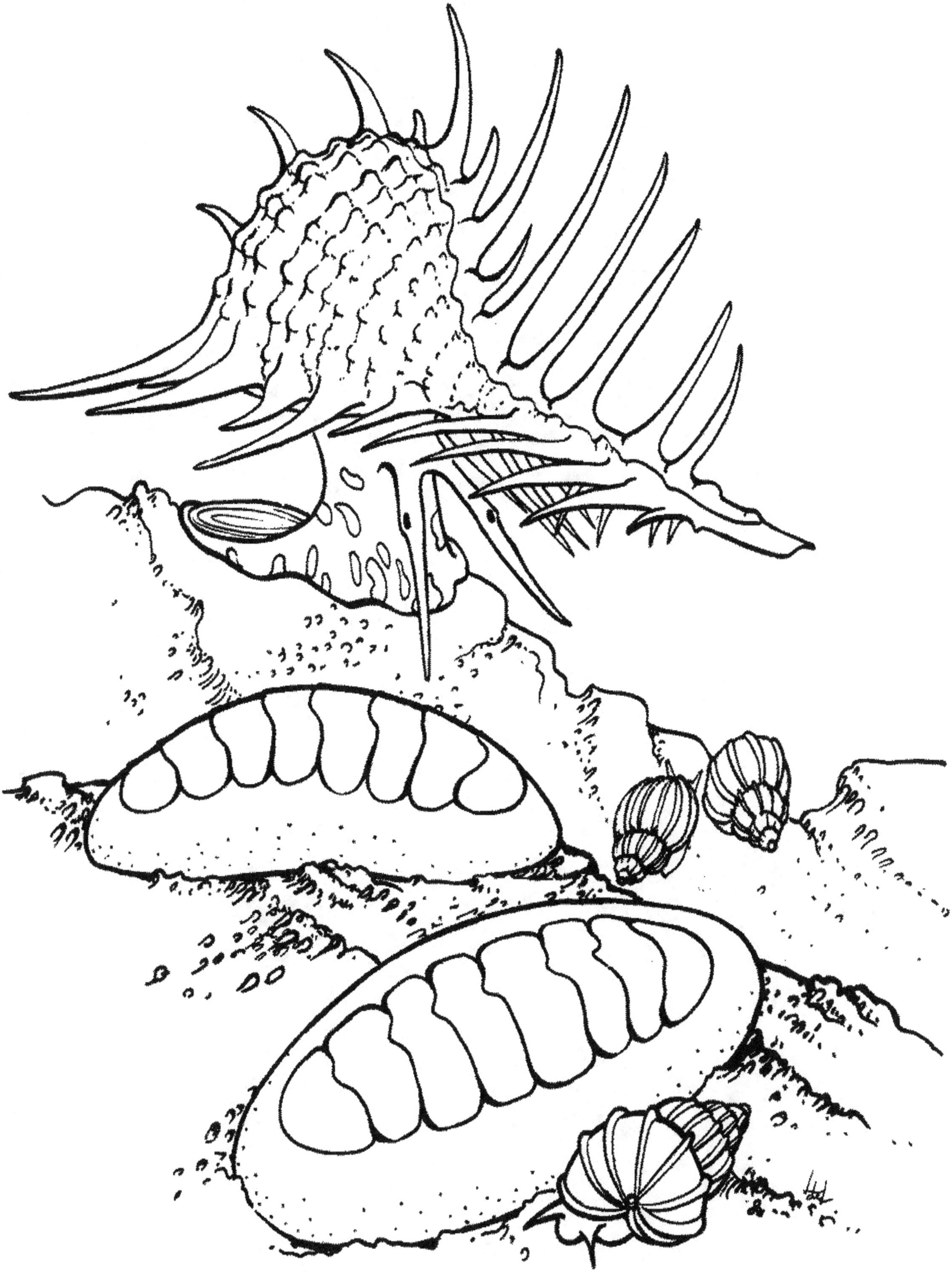

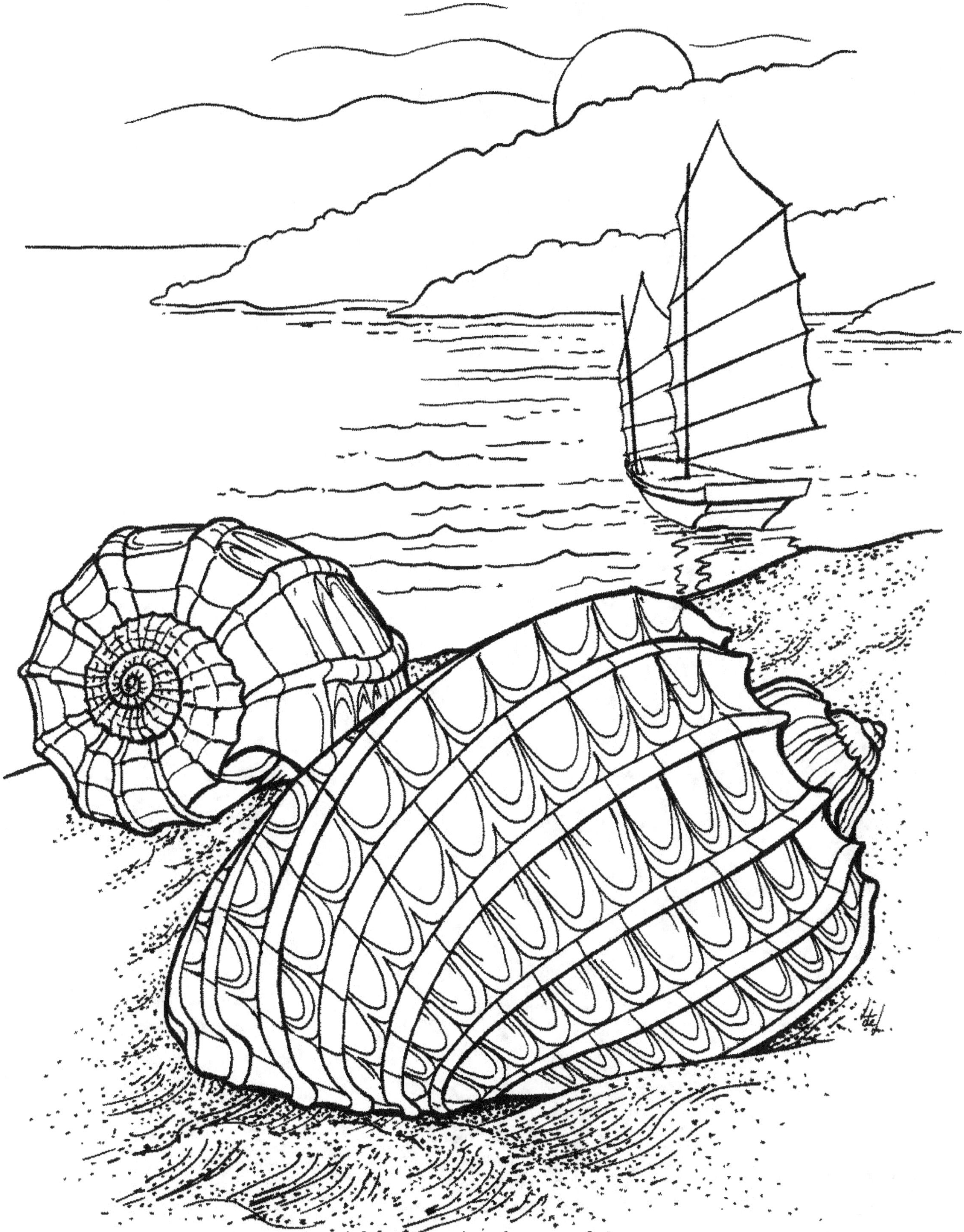

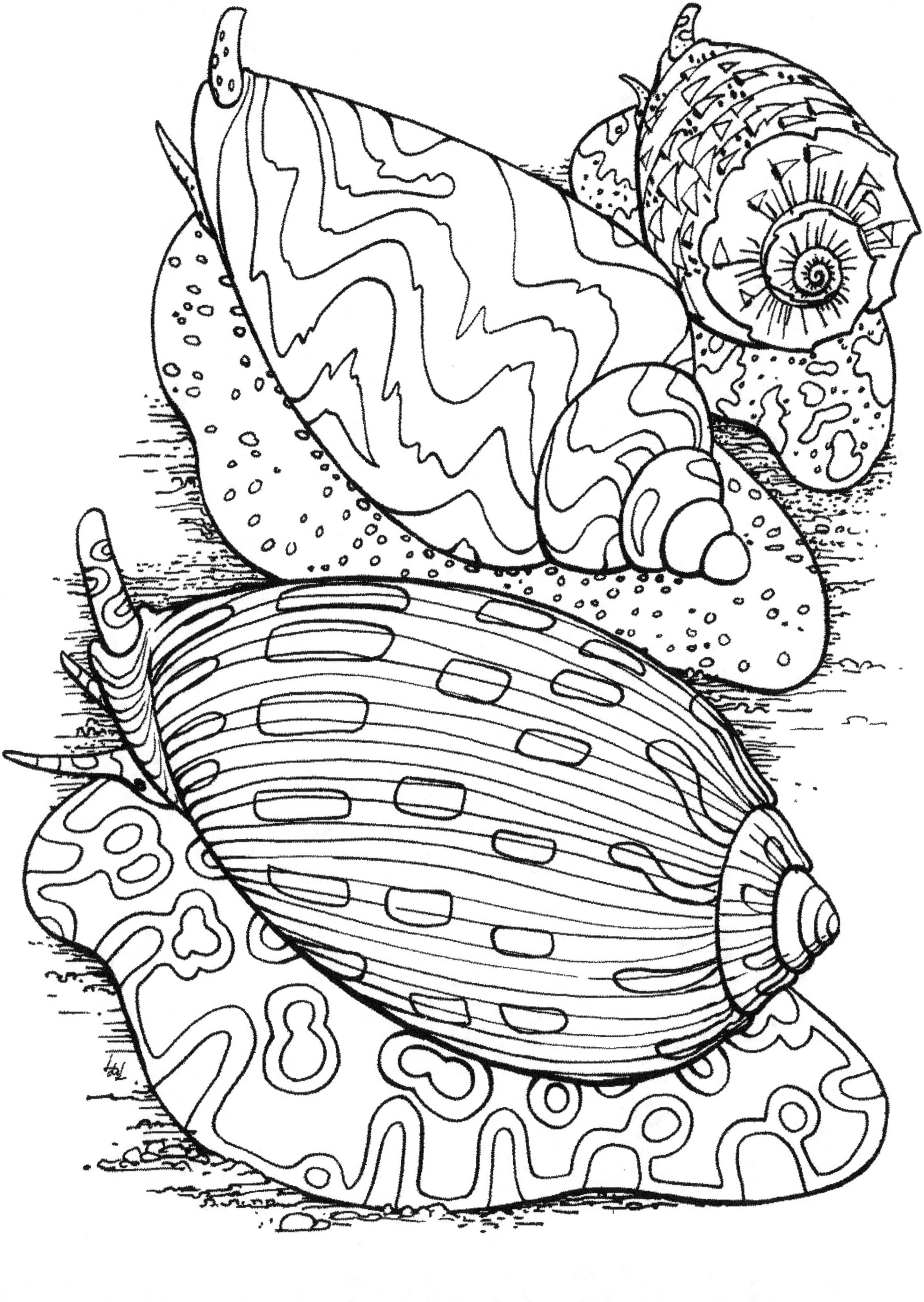

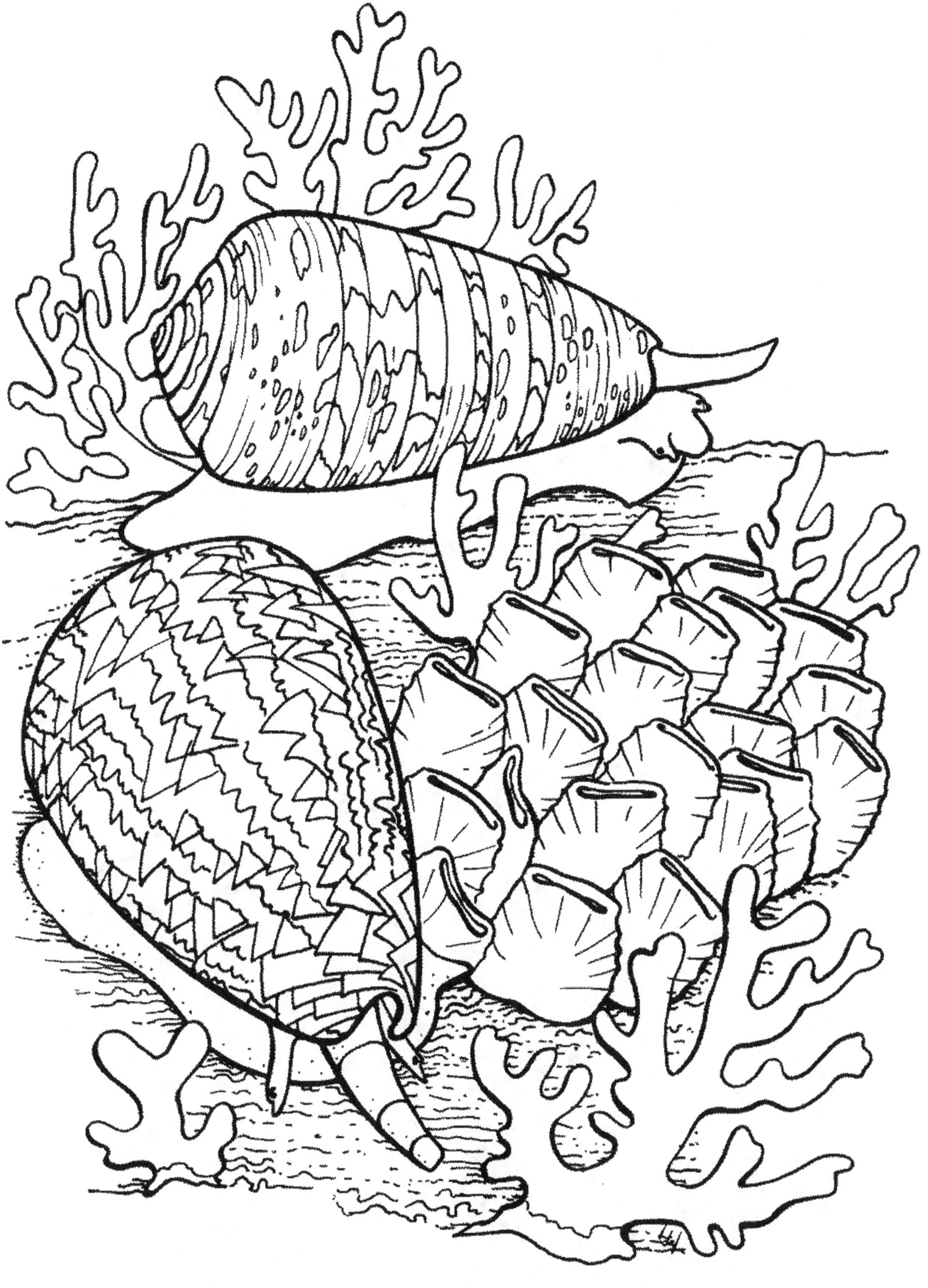

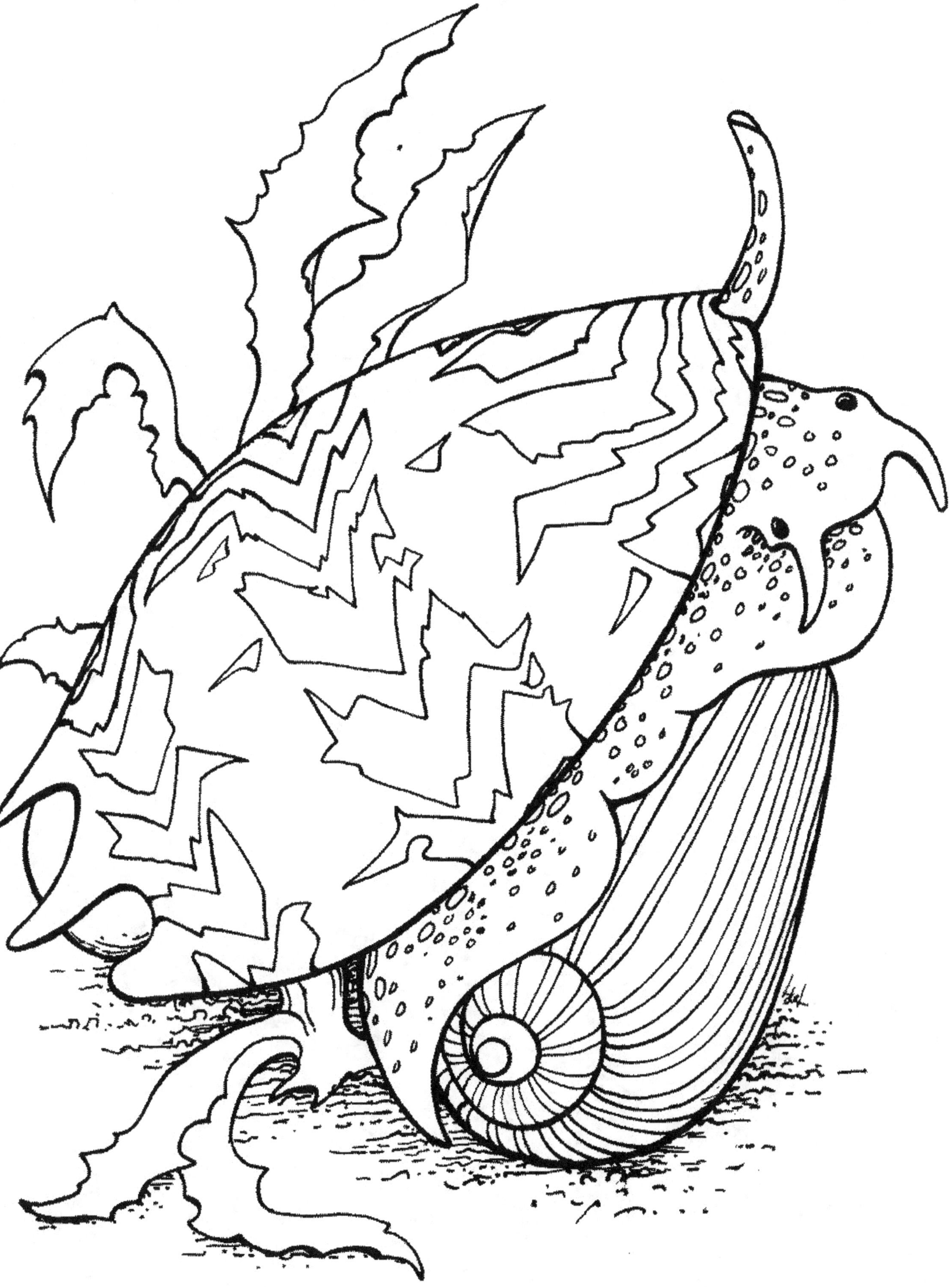

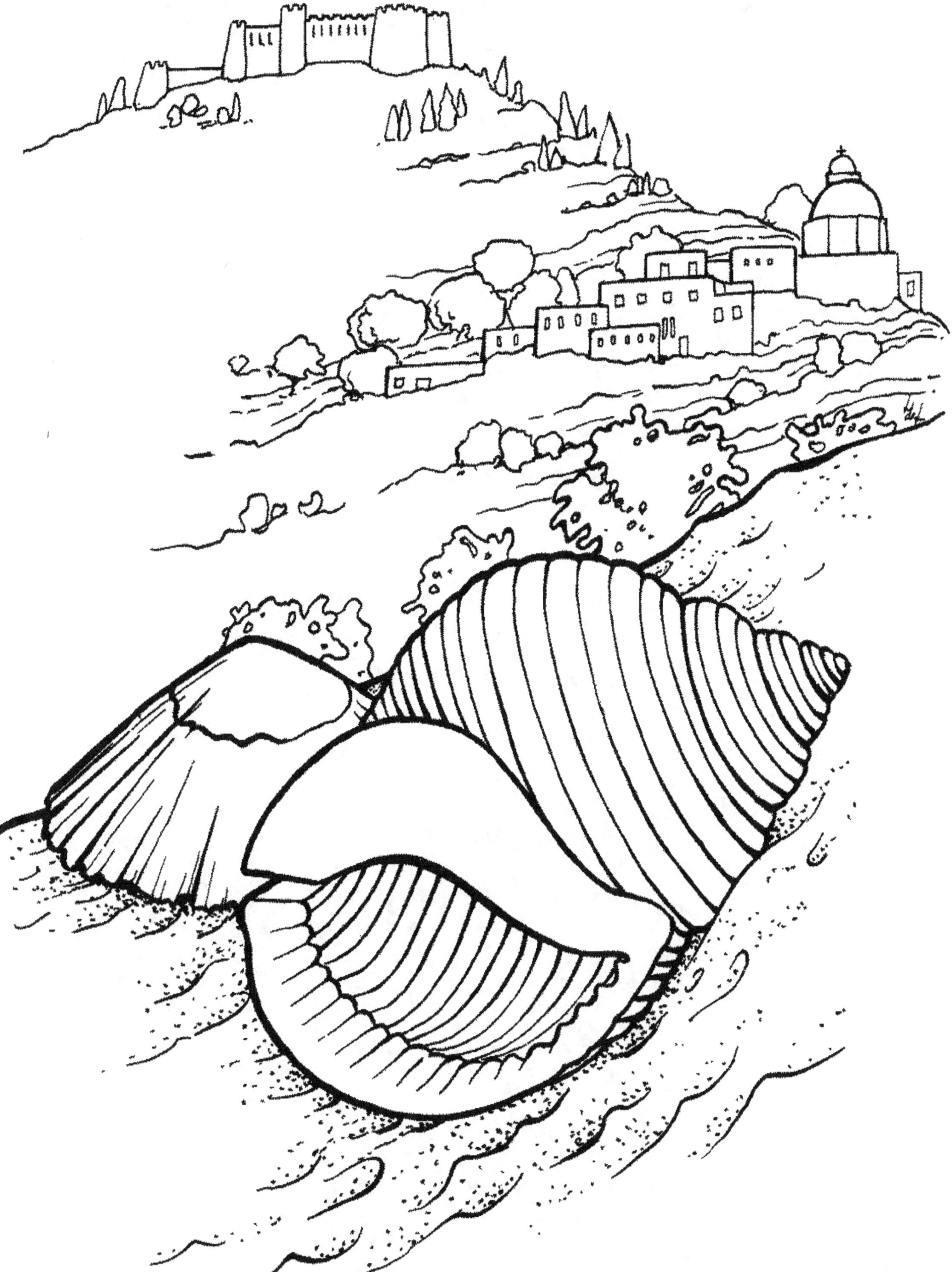

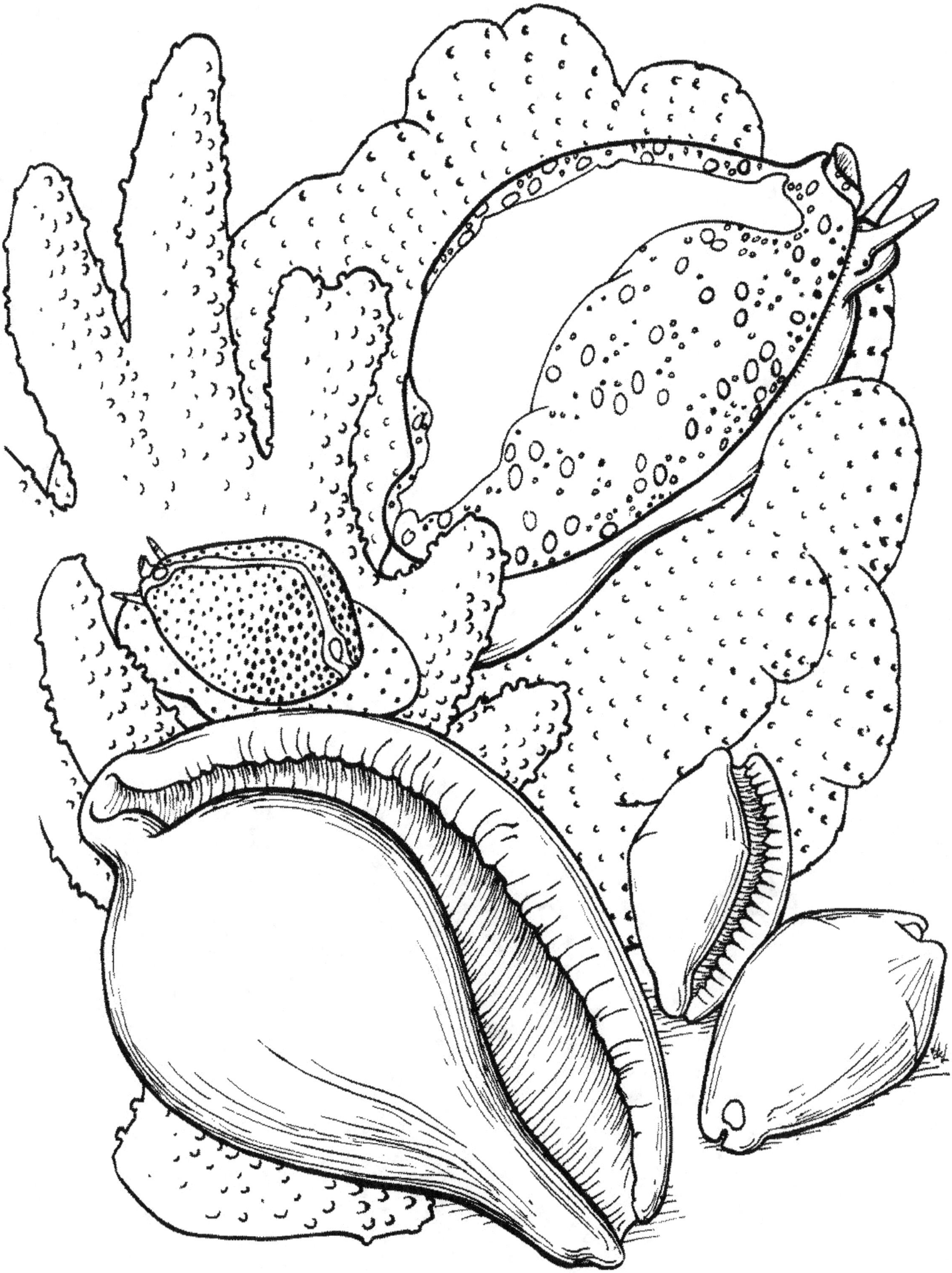

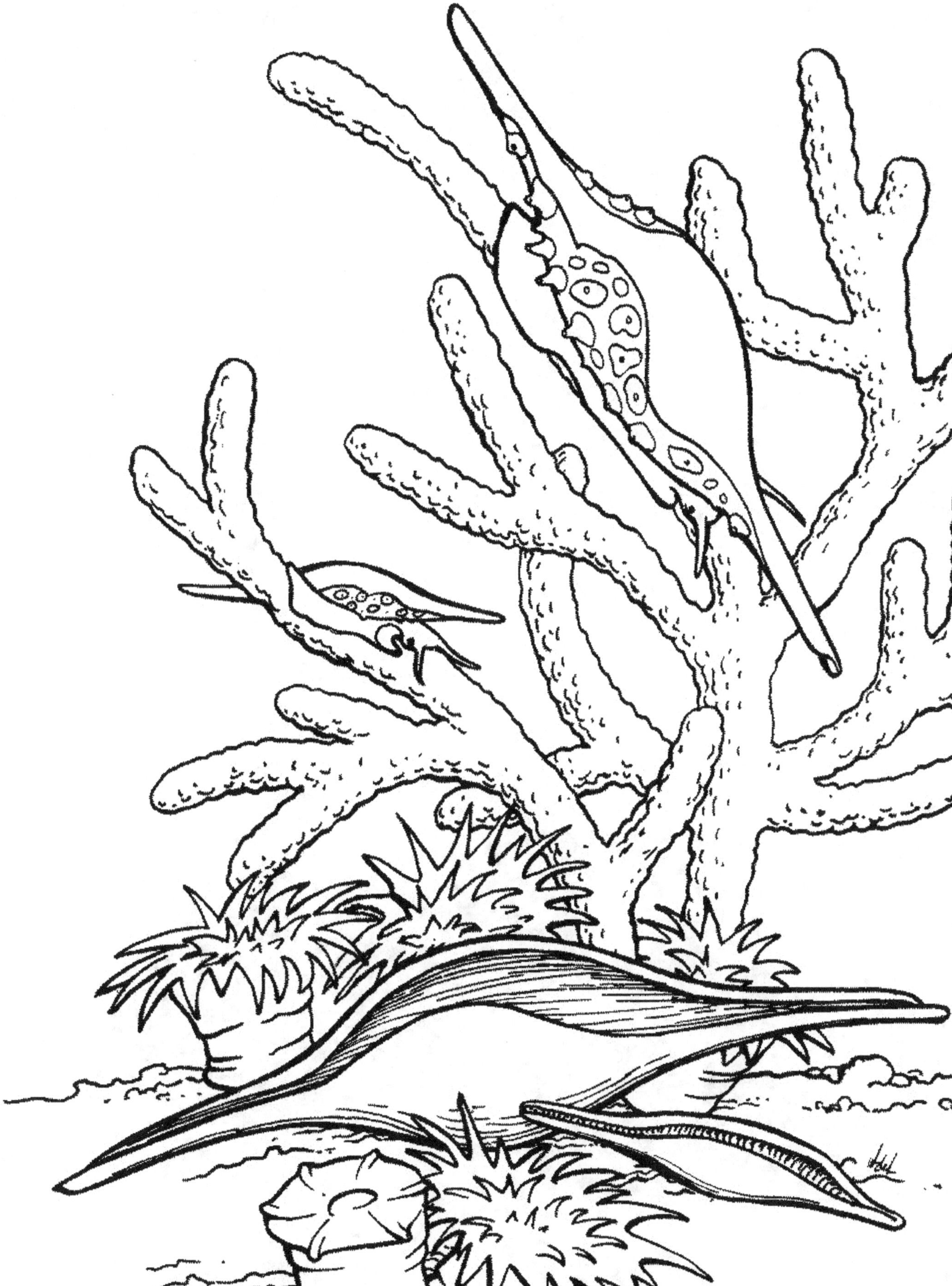

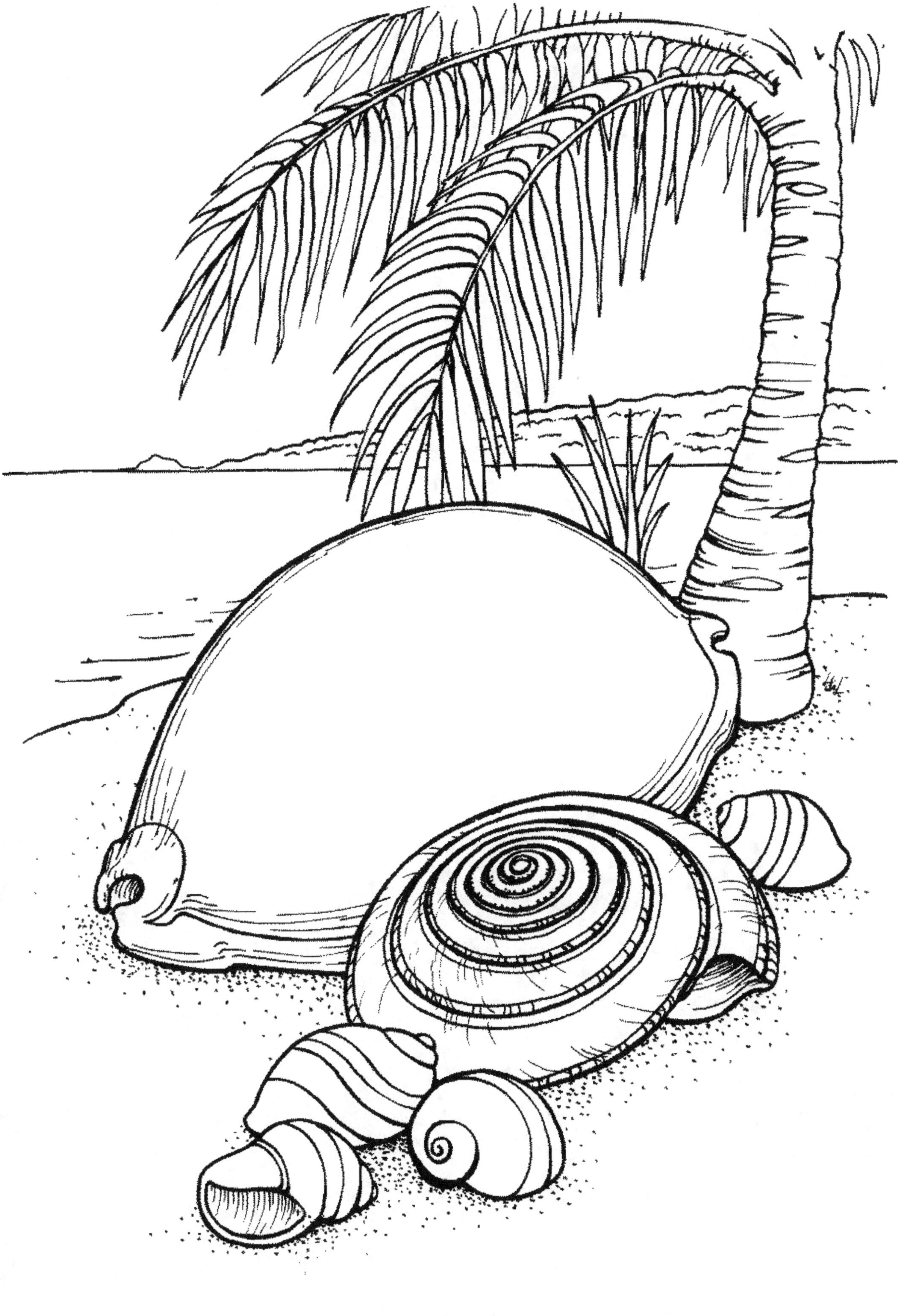

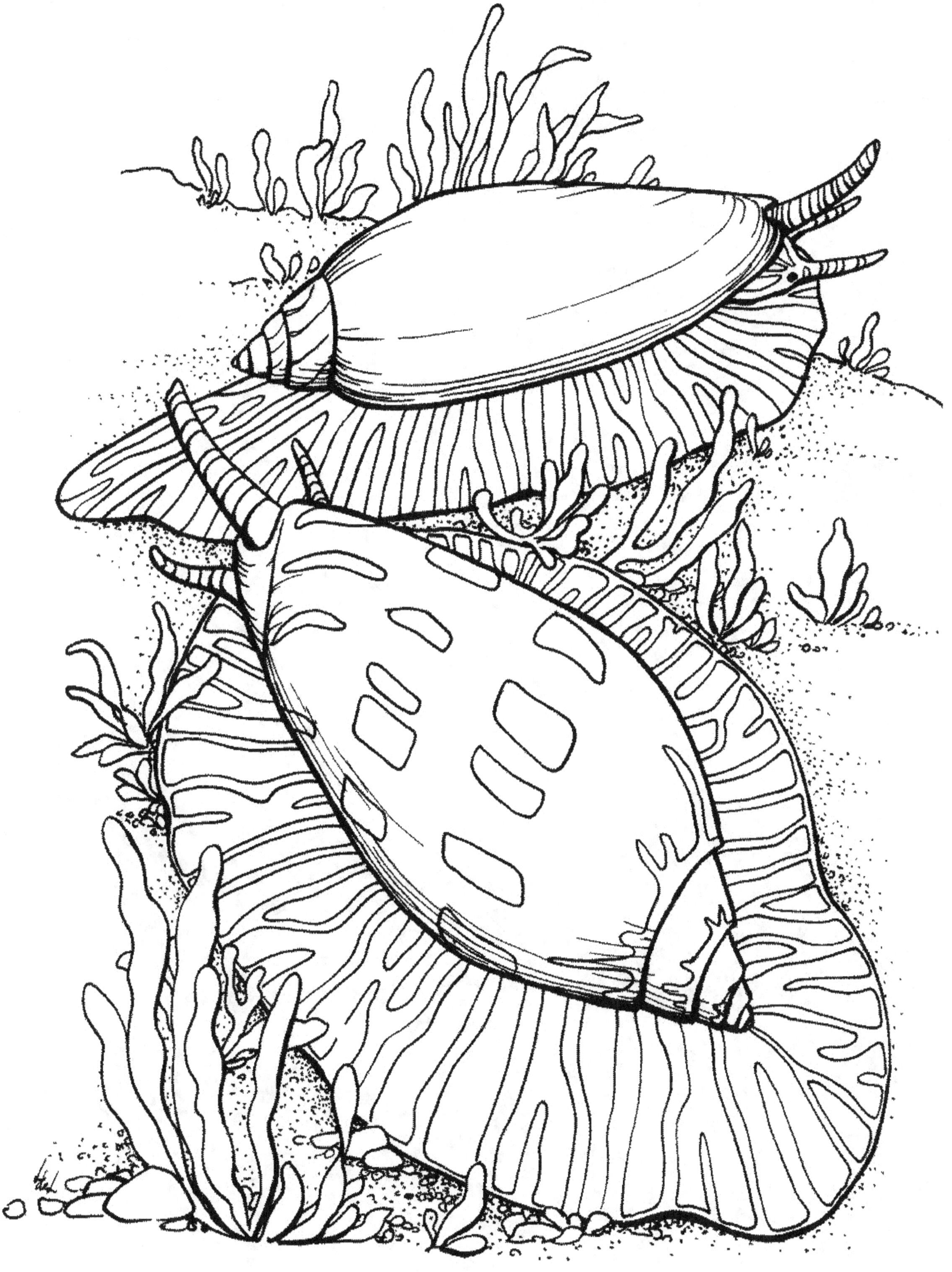

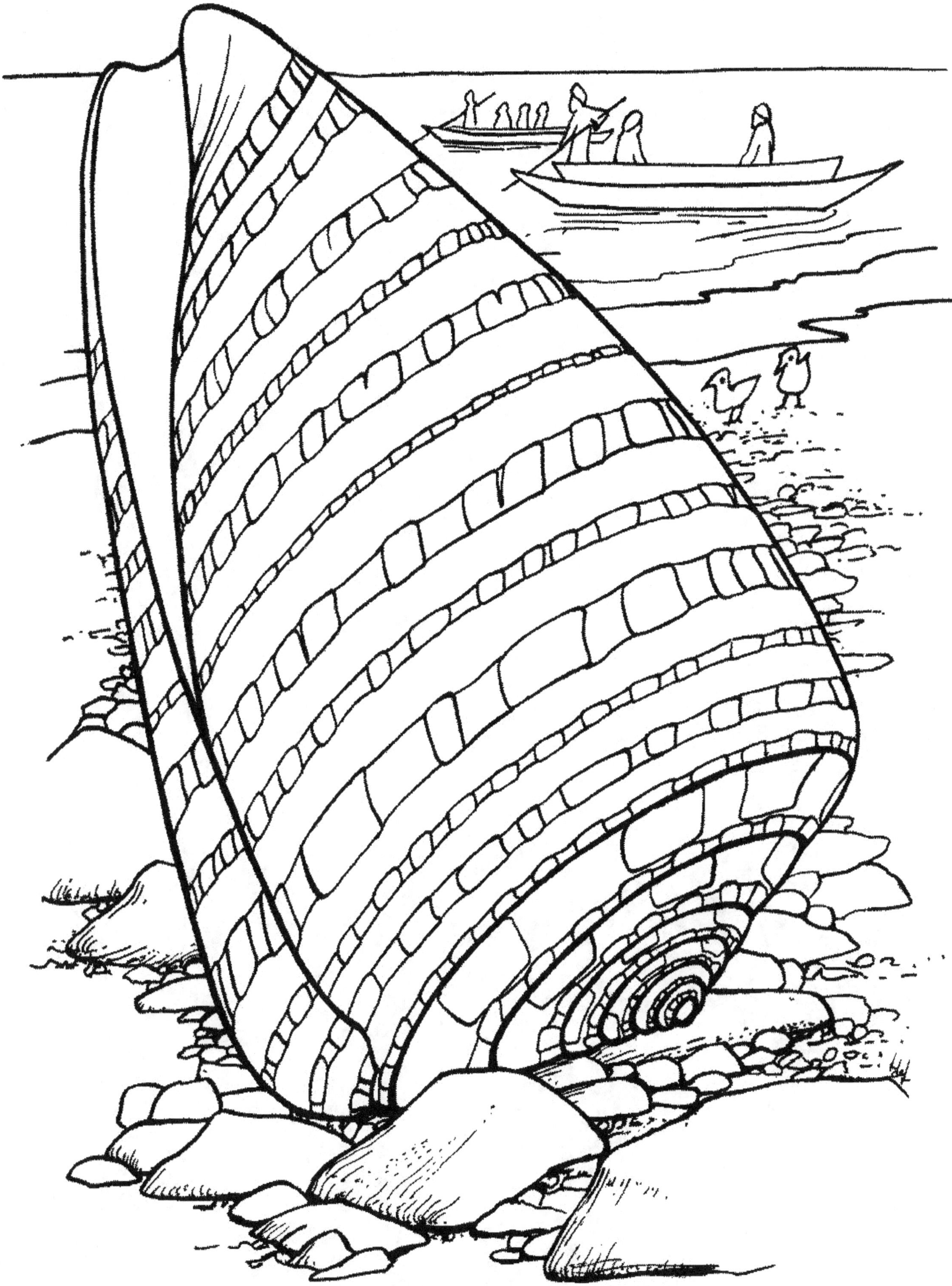

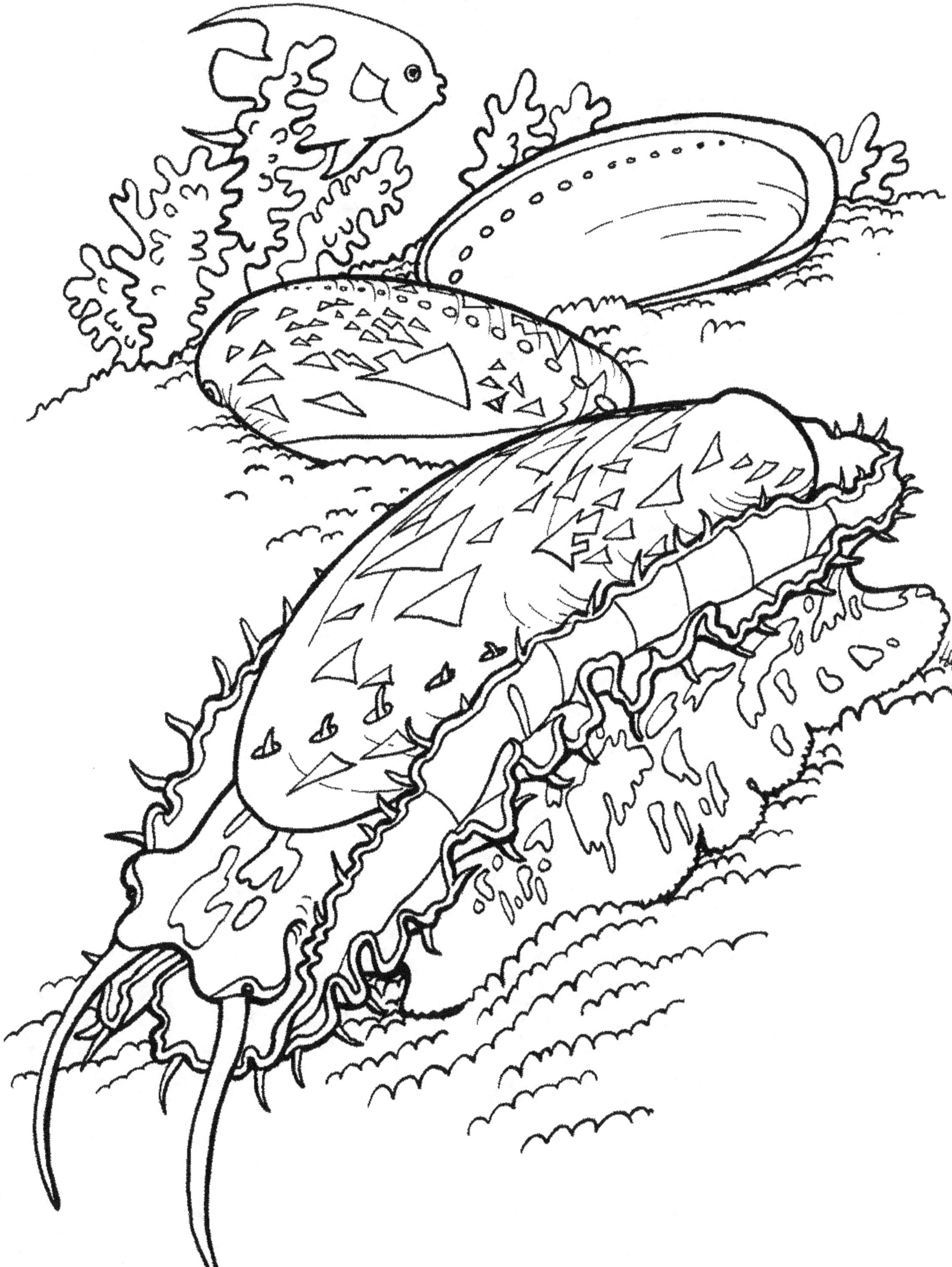

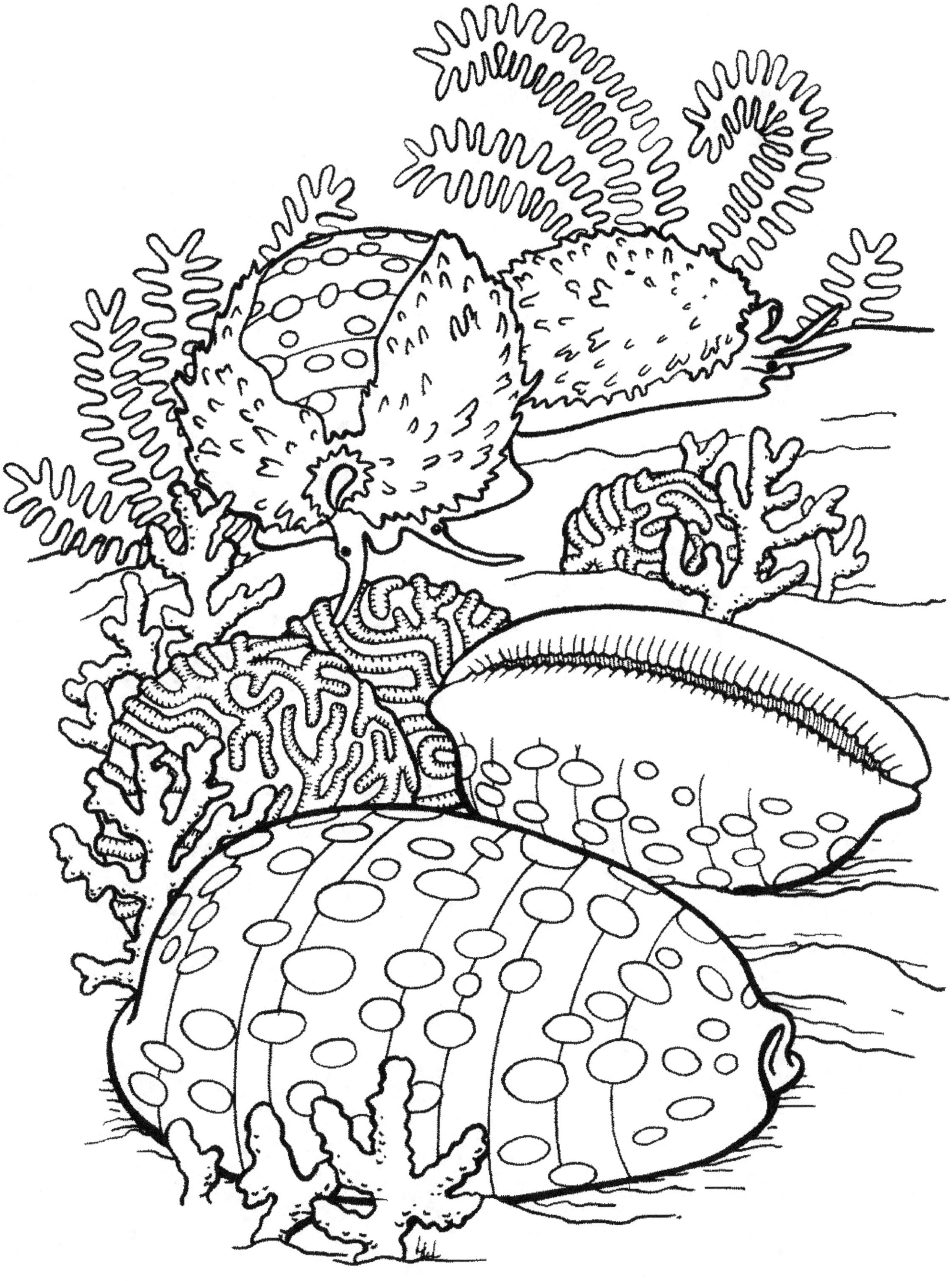

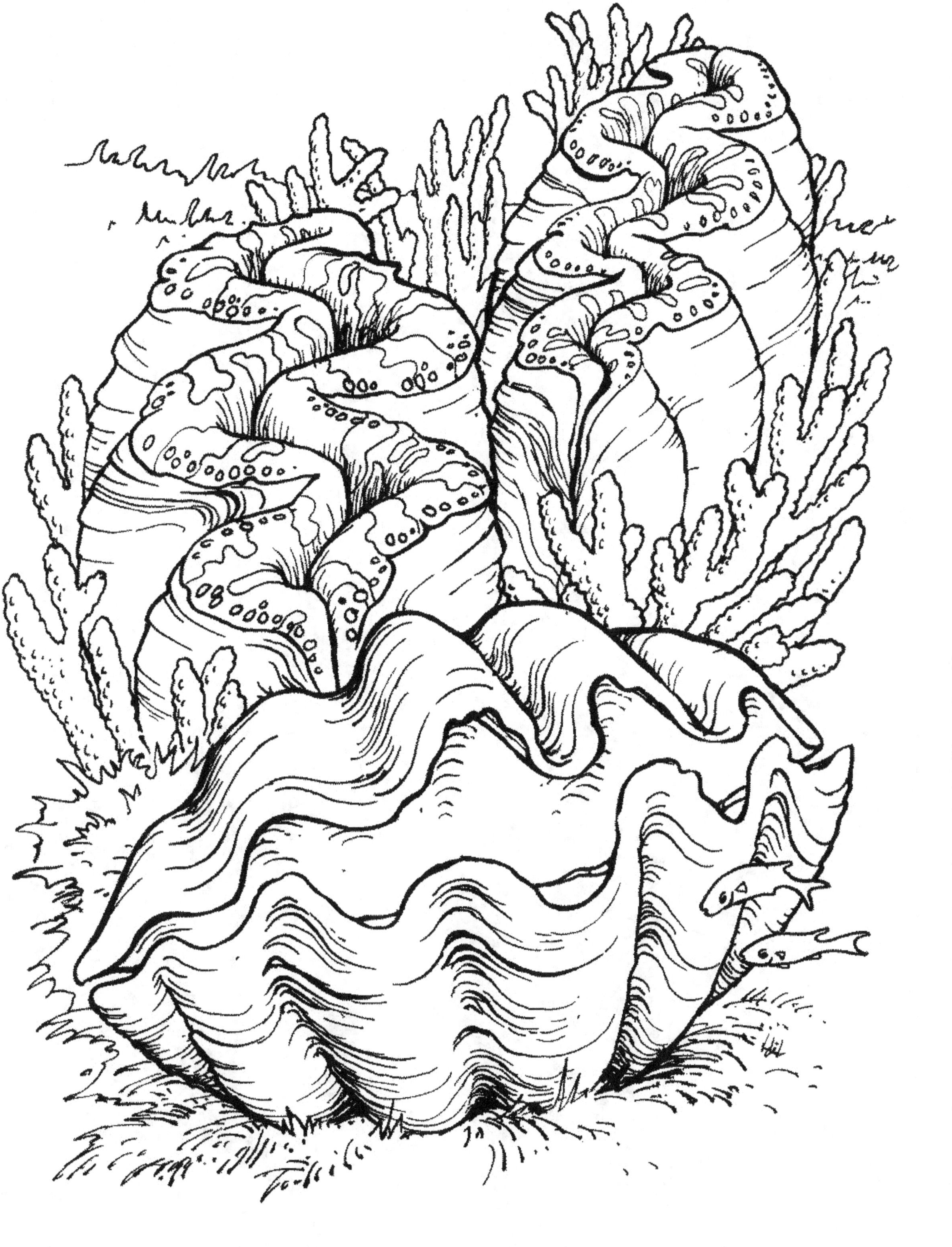

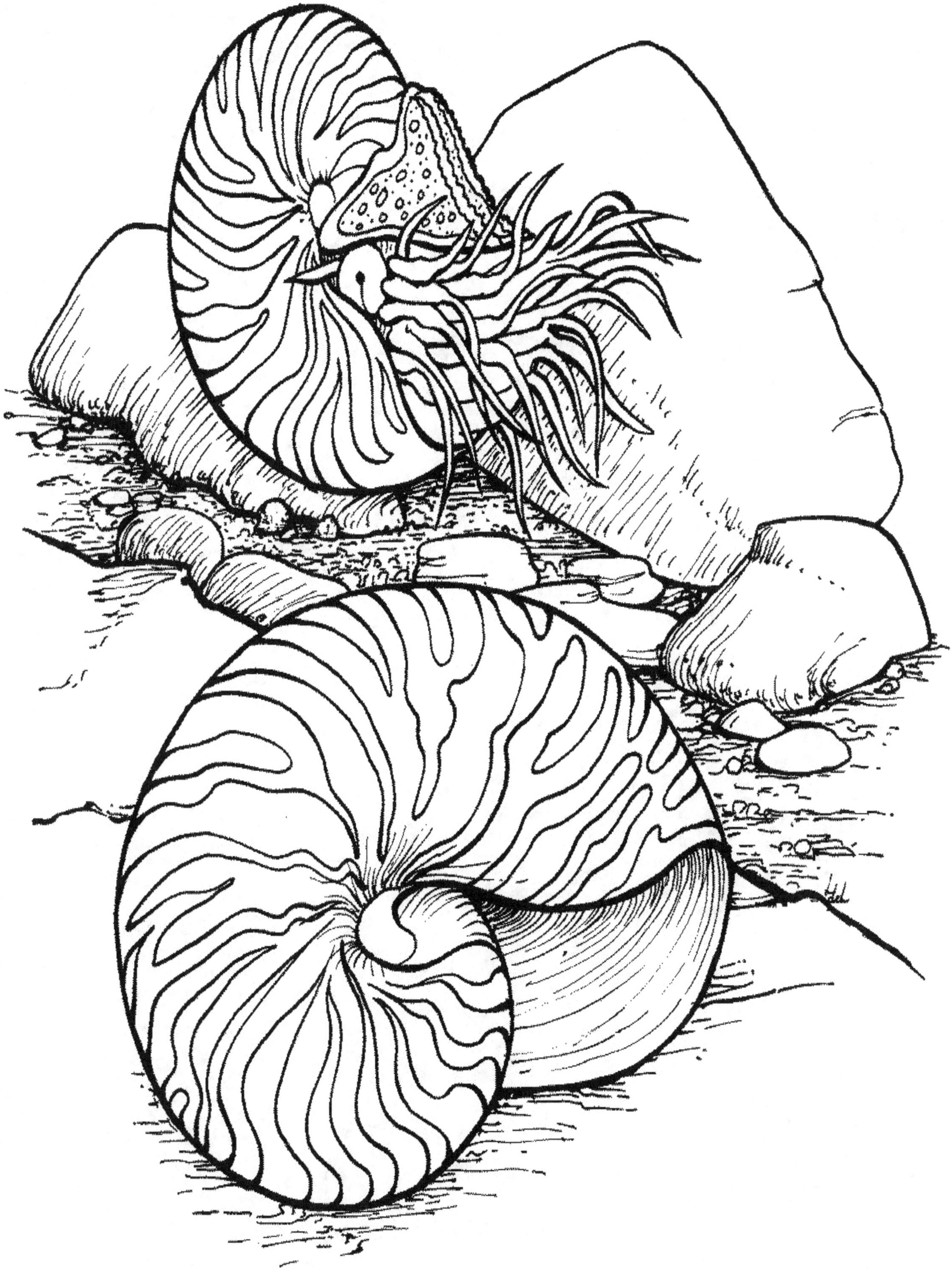

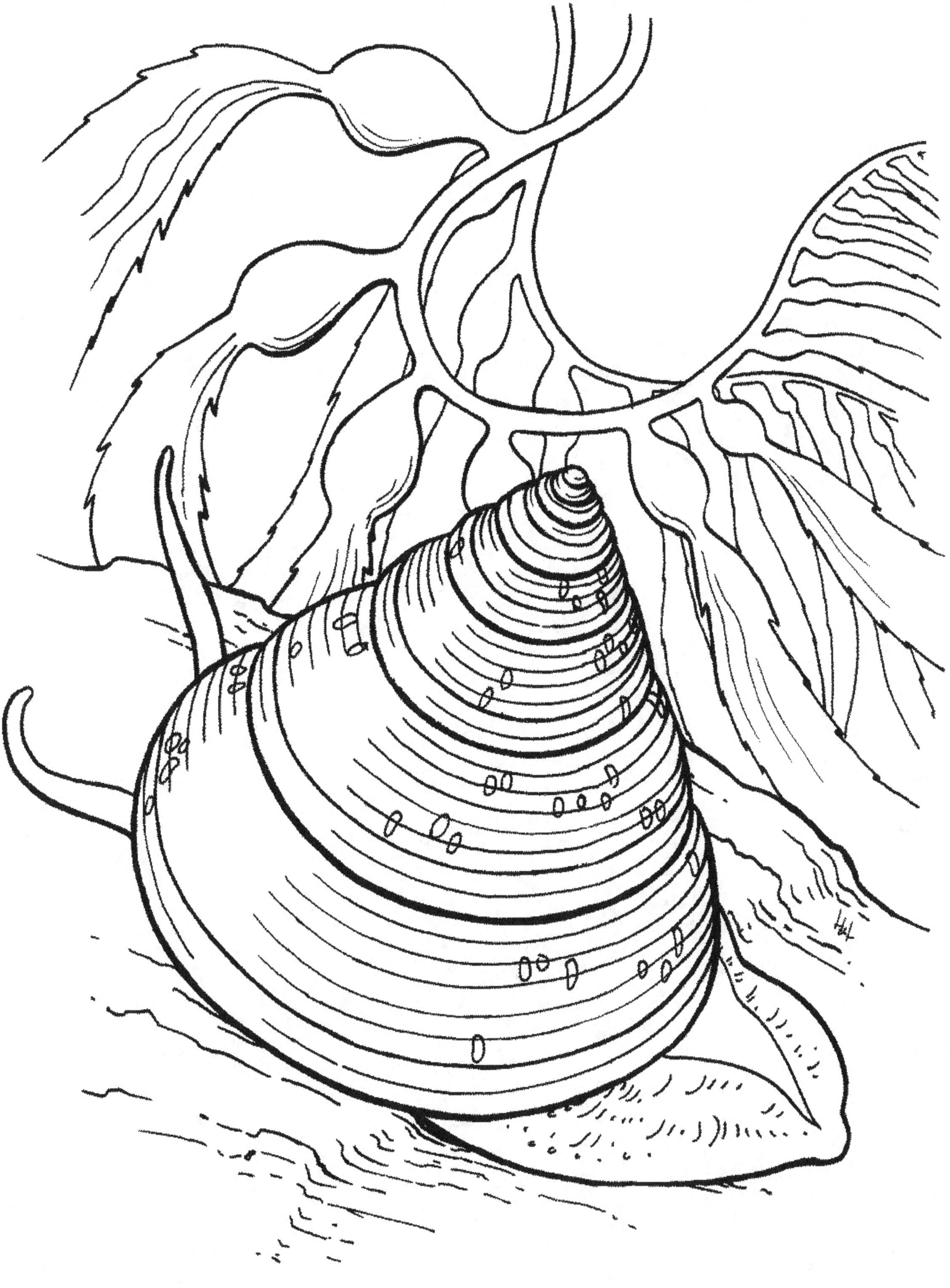

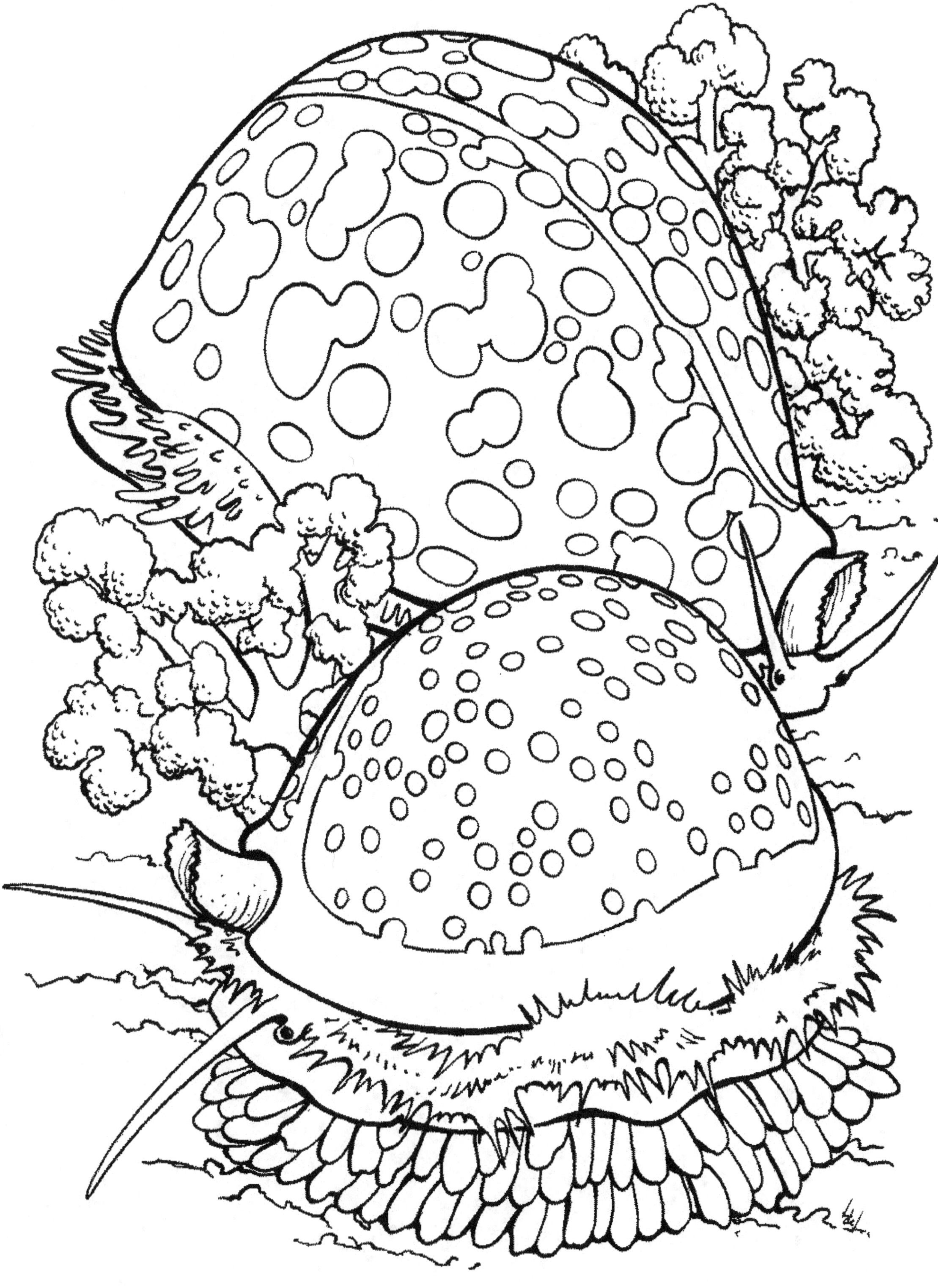

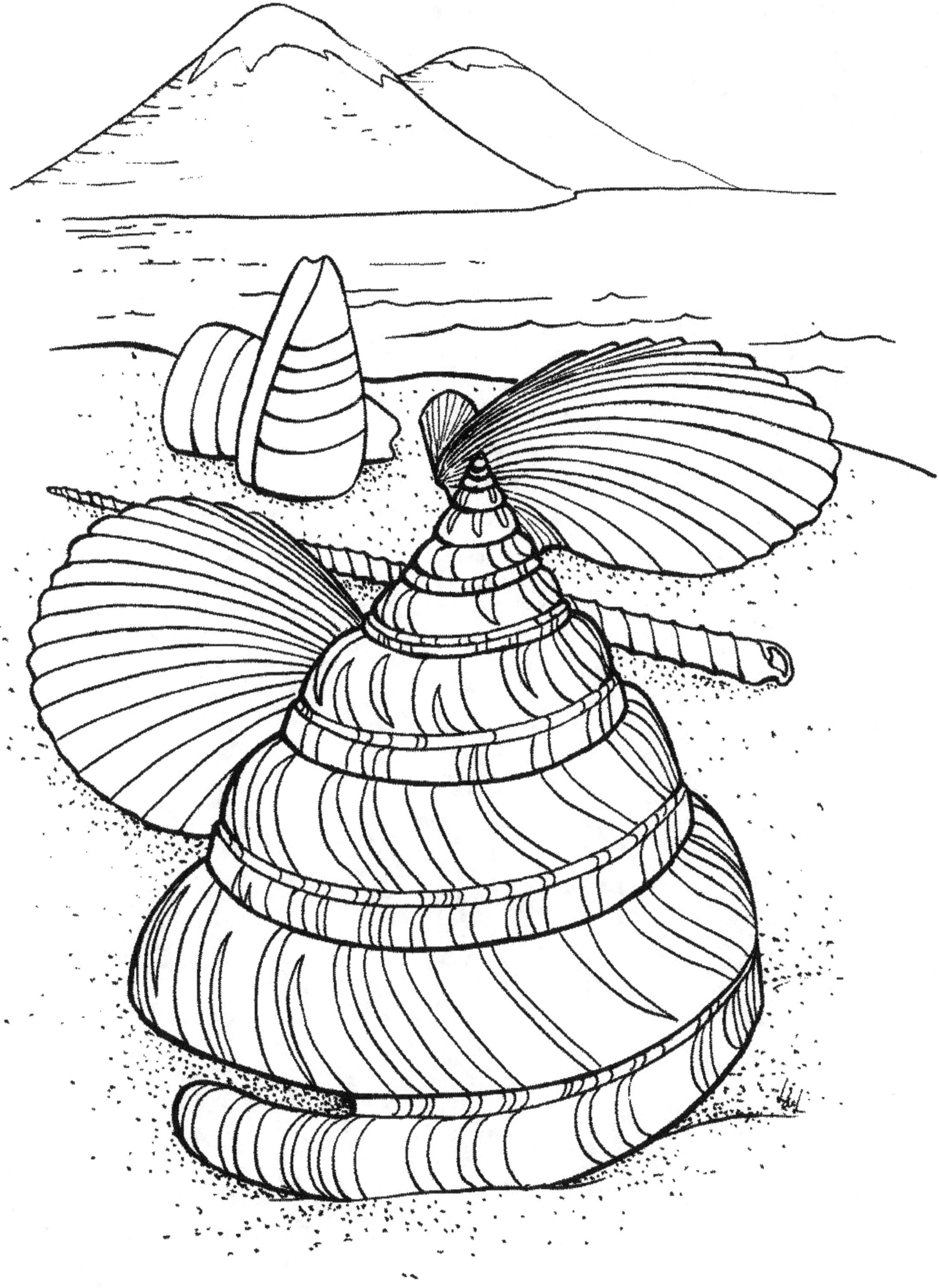

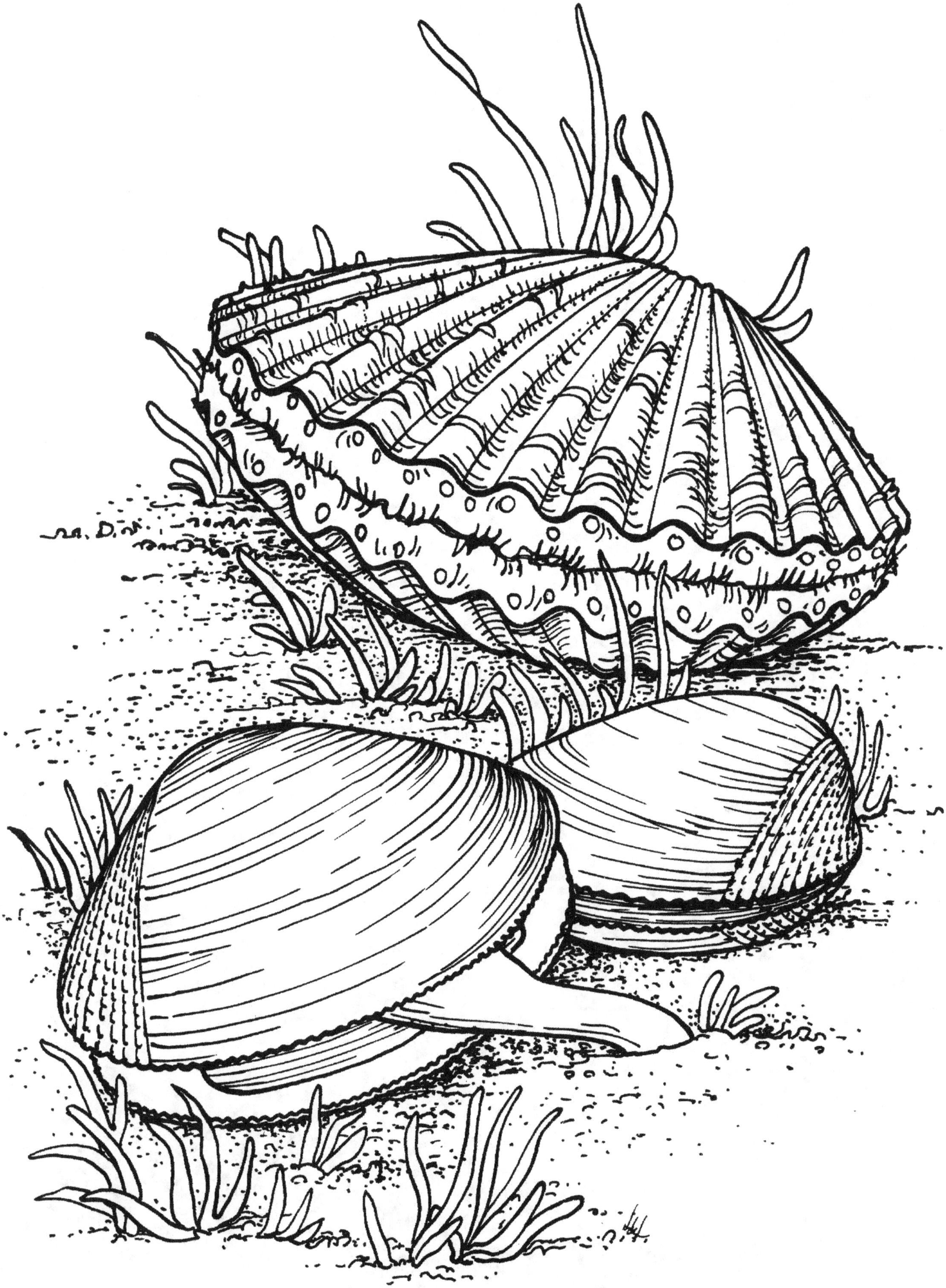

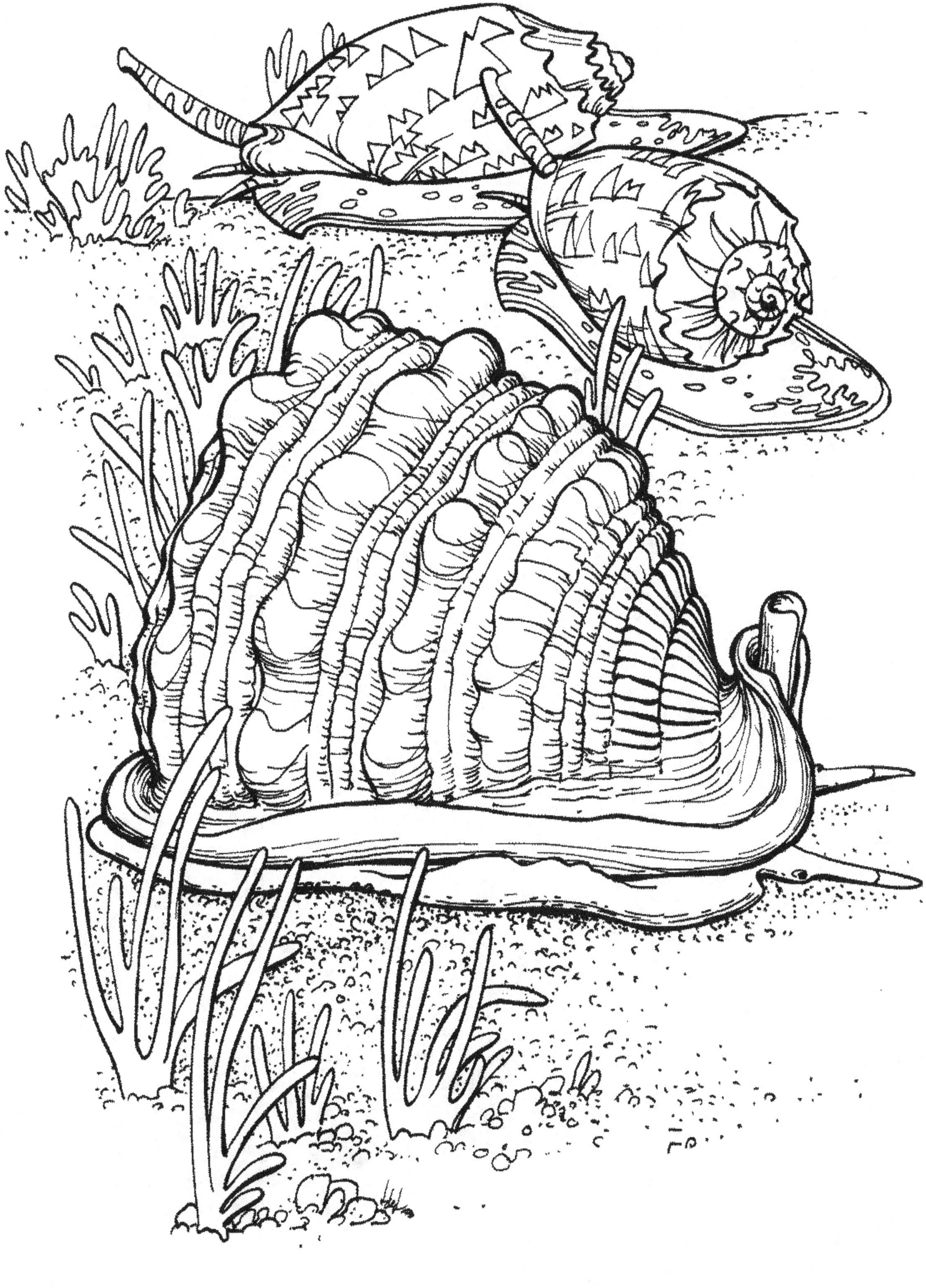

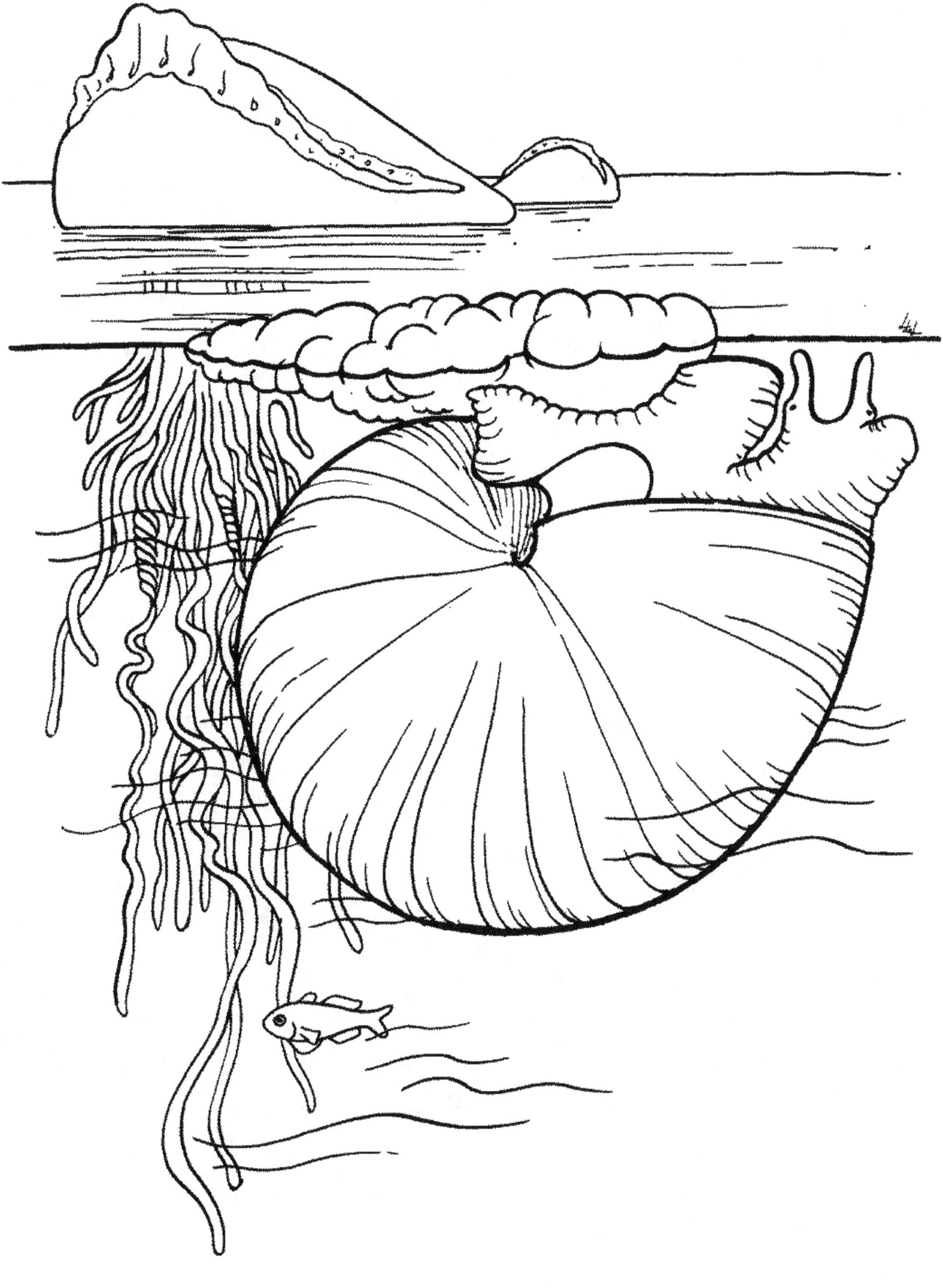

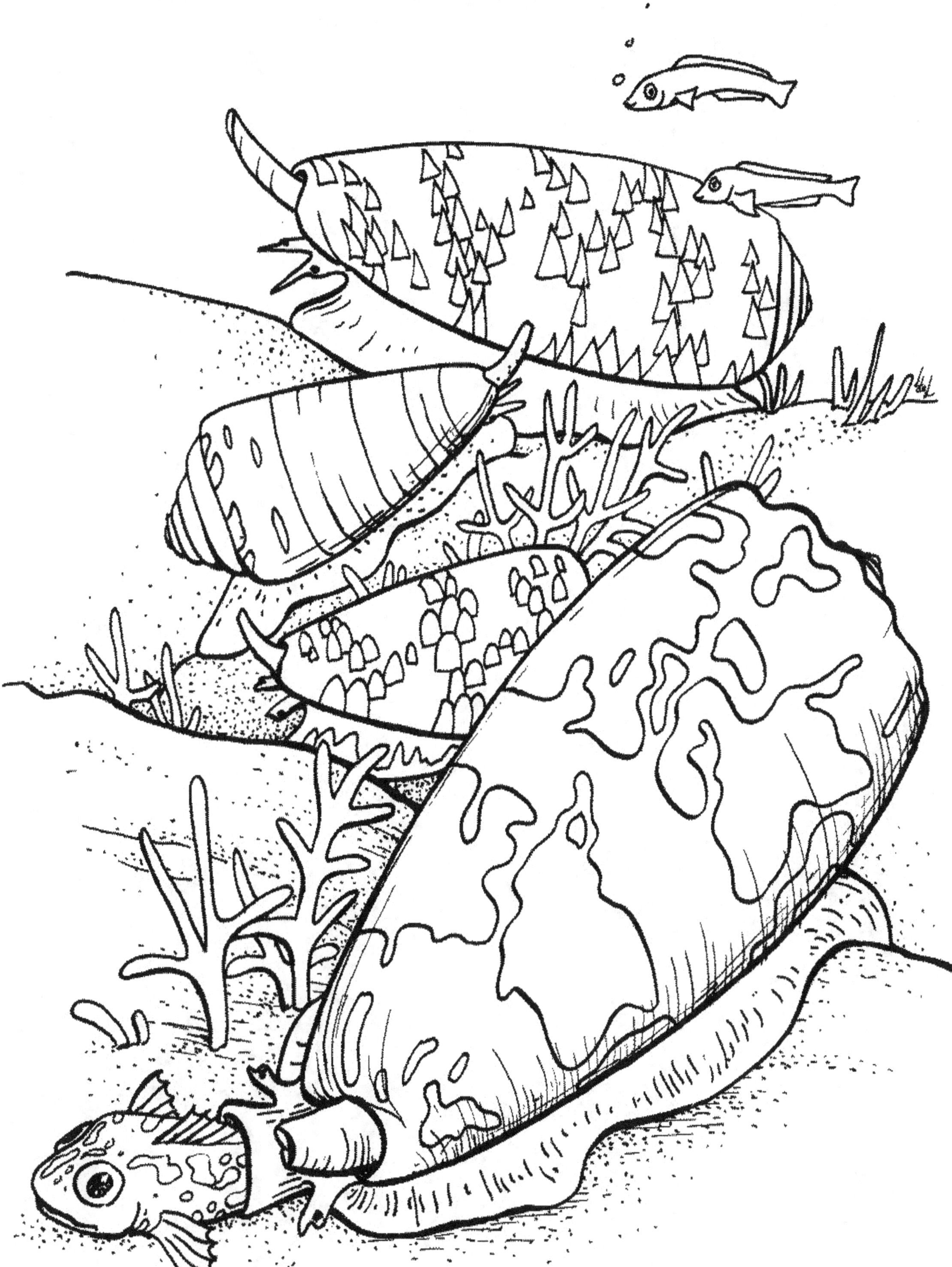

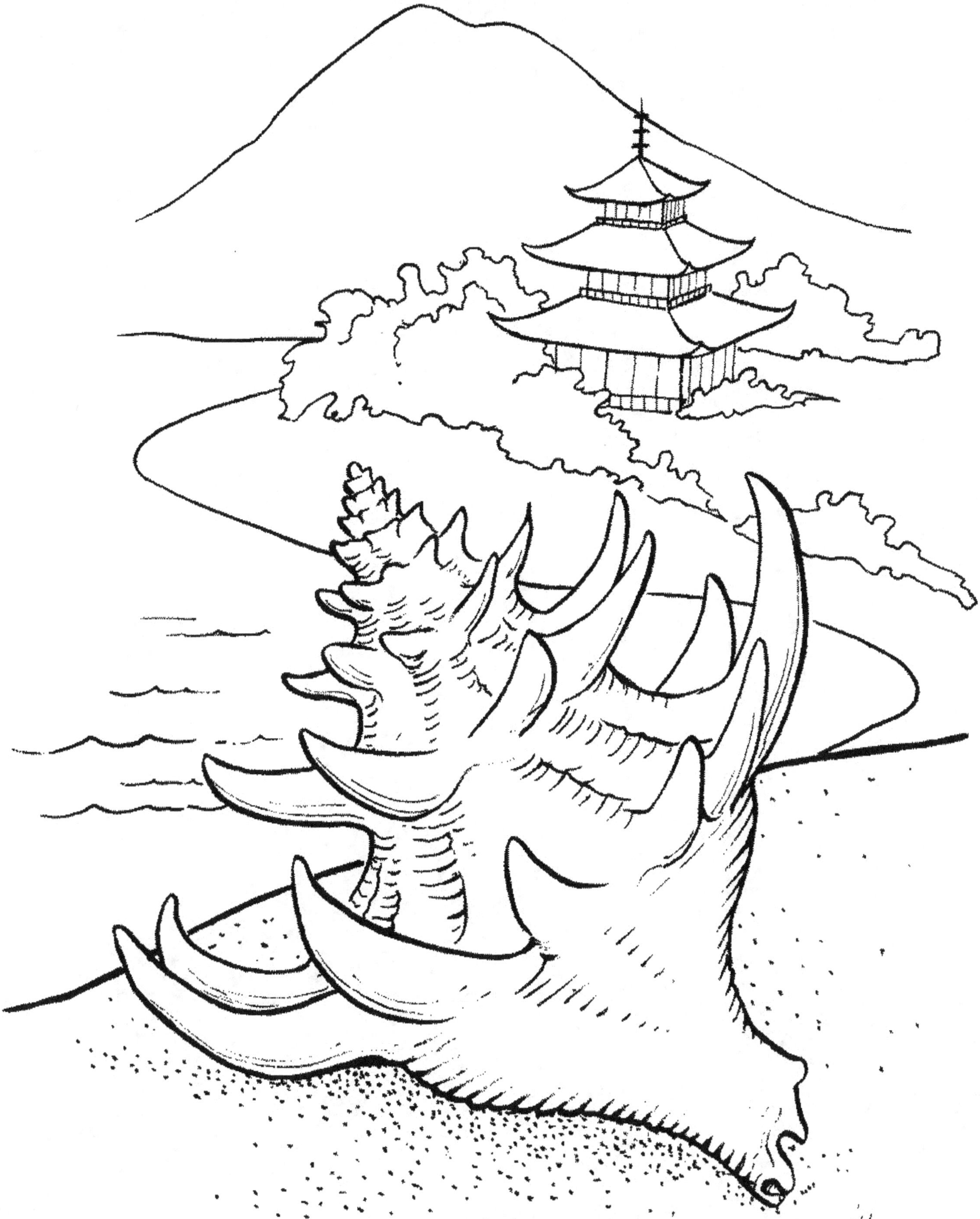

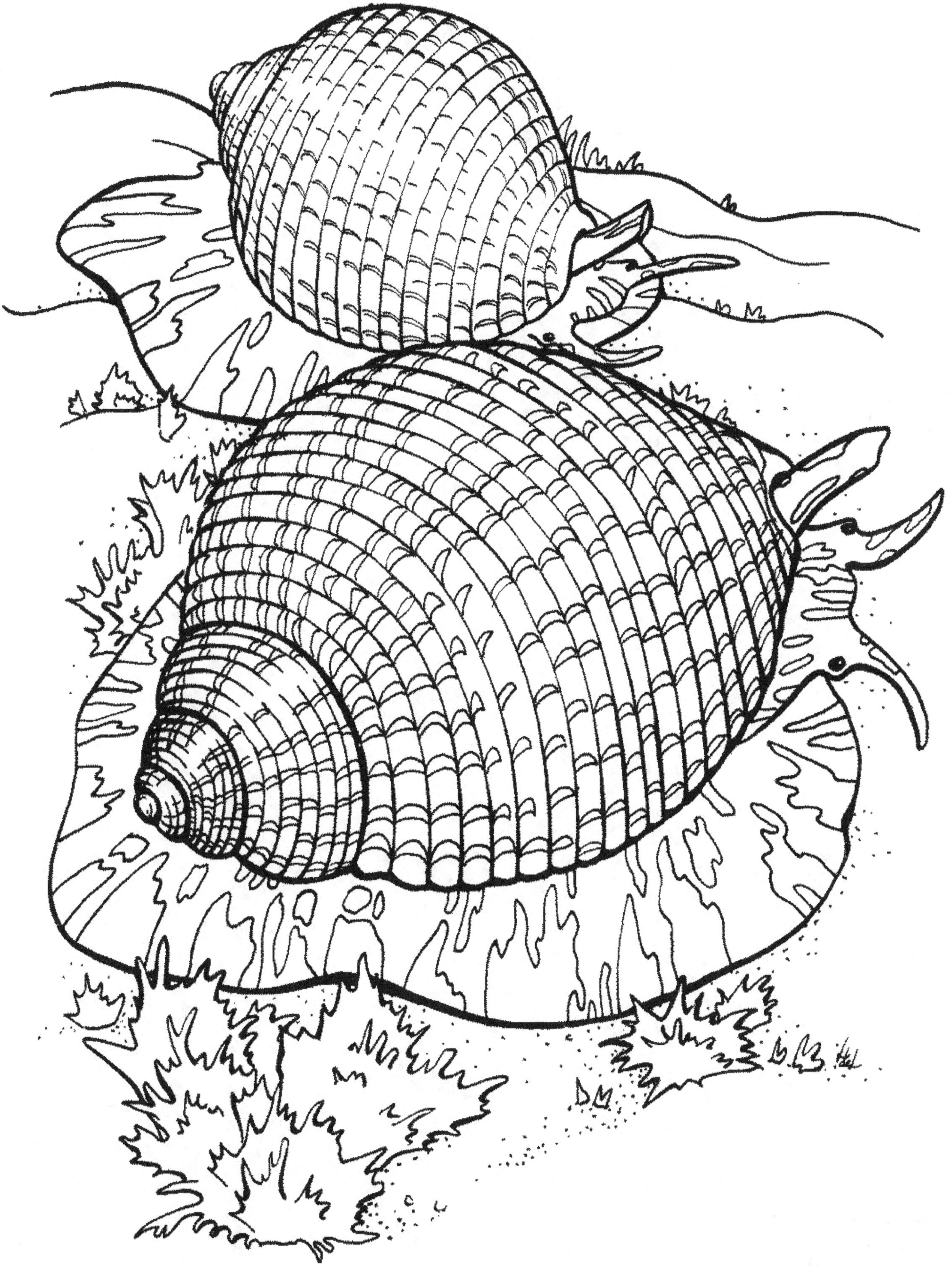

www.ingramcontent.com/pod-product-compliance
Lightning Source LLC
Chambersburg PA
CBHW081530220526
45467CB00010B/3112
* 9 7 8 1 7 1 1 0 5 6 9 9 9 *